IF YOU LIKE
TRUE BLOOD...

IF YOU LIKE

TRUE BLOOD...

HERE ARE **OVER 200** FILMS, TV SHOWS, AND OTHER ODDITIES THAT YOU WILL LOVE

DAVE THOMPSON

Backbeat
Books

AN IMPRINT OF HAL LEONARD CORPORATION

Published in 2013 by Limelight Editions
An Imprint of Hal Leonard Corporation
7777 West Bluemound Road
Milwaukee, WI 53213

Trade Book Division Editorial Offices
33 Plymouth St., Montclair, NJ 07042

Printed in the United States of America

Book design by Michael Kellner

Library of Congress Cataloging-in-Publication Data

Thompson, Dave, 1960 January 3-
    If you like True blood... here are over 200 films, TV shows, and other oddities that you will love / Dave Thompson.
        pages cm
    Includes bibliographical references and index.
    ISBN 978-0-87910-811-3
    1. Vampires in motion pictures. 2. Vampires on television. 3. Horror films--History and criticism. 4. Horror television programs--History and criticism. I. Title.
    PN1995.9.V3T45 2013
    791.43'675--dc23
                                    2013010588

www.limelighteditions.com

CONTENTS

IF YOU LIKE
TRUE
BLOOD...

Spanning some fifteen years from the late 1950s to the early 1970s, the British studio Hammer Films redefined Dracula for the future—as in *Dracula, Prince of Darkness* (1966)—and reinvented a lot of what we expect from vampires as well. (Author's collection)

Introduction

OR, CONFESSIONS OF A
TEENAGED VAMPIRE HUNTER

It's a simple premise and, if you want to read between the cultural lines, a timely one too. An entire subsection of society, hitherto living so far below the radar that most folk don't even know it exists, comes collectively "out of the closet"—and the rest of the country has to figure out what to do with it. Especially as, in this case, the closet is actually (or, at least, figuratively) a casket, and far from being a subsection, this new society is more ancient, and more widespread, than anybody could ever have imagined.

That is the story behind *True Blood*, an HBO TV series since 2008, but before that a series of Southern Vampire mysteries penned by novelist Charlaine Harris since 2001. At the time of writing, the story has unfurled over twelve breathless volumes, and Harris has admitted it's going to be difficult to wrap up every one of the plot lines in what she has always insisted would be the final (thirteenth) book. But no matter how Sookie Stackhouse's journey may end, the mysteries were long ago firmly established as the most believable—and incredible—vampire story in an era that sometimes seems to be overflowing with the things.

The show, like the novels, is the story of one woman in one place: Sookie Stackhouse, a waitress at a bar in the Louisiana backwater of Bon Temps who just happens to fall in lust and love with the first vampire anyone in the town has ever encountered, a Civil War–era gent named Bill Compton. He is drawn to the bar because it's the only place around where they might possibly serve the artificial blood drink that allows vampires to flourish without draining humans. She is drawn to him because he's cute.

It is through Compton that Sookie, Bon Temps, and we the readers and viewers become acquainted with the lives, loves, struggles, and strivings of the vamps, as they in turn learn to take their own place in our world. Conflicts and clashes familiar from countless movements in our own world scar and mar the general belief that we should all get along with one another; there are antivampire humans and antihuman vamps, and if you think gay marriage is a hot political potato, wait until mixed-species marriage hits the Hill.

But it's not only vampires with which this new world has to contend. For no sooner have the vampires stepped out of the legends that they themselves constructed to hide their existence from humankind than a wealth of other beings emerge from the supernatural shadowlands. Shapeshifters, werewolves, fairies, witches— weirdness of every variety piles out of mankind's mythology to work its magic or make general mayhem, and not only with the unsuspecting mortals. Sookie turns out to be descended from fairies, Elvis is revealed to be a vampire, and history is turned upside down as religion, science, and culture itself are stripped bare of the most precious conceits. And the fresh mythologies that Harris weaves around her universe swiftly become as believable (or otherwise) as any that our own world has constructed around the supernatural world. Sometimes even more so.

But the stories (like their inhabitants) did not emerge out of a vacuum, and if you like *True Blood*, chances are, you are already familiar with a lot of their antecedents. You might even, in fact, have lived one or two. Vampires do not merely stalk the pages of fiction, after all. As I write these words in early 2013, the news wires hum with tales of a real-life vampire scare haunting the Serbian village of Zarozje after the collapse of an old haunted mill apparently disturbed the slumbers of Sava Savanovic, Serbia's most famous vampire.

Of course we can scoff and say Serbia is far away and vampire legends are ten-a-penny there. Just forty years ago, however, a similar horror was said to stalk somewhat closer to home, in the city of London, England. And if I were of a more fanciful mind, I could even say I got my own first taste of true blood there. I didn't, but I could.

Highgate Cemetery is surely the most famous necropolis in the world. Others may be more historic; others still may be more haunted. And others again may have a more distinguished registry of residents. But still, Highgate has an aura and a reputation that are second to none, whether as the last resting place of the philosopher Karl Marx or as the immutable centerpiece to Audrey Niffenegger's *Her Fearful Symmetry*, one of *the* most deservedly acclaimed supernatural novels of the century-so-far.

Niffenegger herself described Highgate as "a high-walled secret garden of death," and in an interview with *The Guardian*, quoted another (unnamed) visitor's prosaic "[a] jungle inside a forest." But she was merely the latest in a procession of creative minds to be drawn to Highgate. The child vampire Lucy Westenra was buried here in Bram Stoker's *Dracula* (Stoker changed the cemetery's name to Eaststead, but it is unmistakable regardless), drifting wraithlike along the winding, overgrown pathways, seeking new playmates for her immortal appetites. And close to seventy years later, the Hammer movie studio's *Taste the Blood of Dracula* included several scenes shot in the graveyard.

Because if any burial ground *should* be stalked by a vampire, it's Highgate. Located in North London and divided between the West and East cemeteries, the graveyard sprawls, shadowy and overgrown, for at least a couple of days' worth of exploration. Opened in 1839, it is scarcely an ancient burial ground, not like some of those you can find around the UK. But it feels like one, and even the most down-to-earth visitor is likely to feel at least a passing thrill when crossing through—a thrill that is only amplified when you recall the cemetery's best-known supernatural occupant.

The Highgate Cemetery Vampire's reign of something-not-quite-approaching-terror caused such a ripple in the more populist British newspapers of 1969–1970 that his legend remains one of the area's most tantalizing tales. So tantalizing that, one summer night in 1975, fifteen-year-old me and a handful of friends met up, armed ourselves with garlic, stakes, silver crucifixes and sundry other death-dealing paraphernalia, and prepared ourselves for a night of fearless vampire hunting.

Or maybe not so fearless. I'd recently watched Roman Polanski's movie of almost the same name (*The Fearless Vampire Killers*) and had been chilled to the bone by the emergence of the most terrifying vamp of them all, as played by actor Alfie Bass. Poised to attack, he is utterly unperturbed by his victim's raising of a crucifix. "Wrong vampire," he laughs. Bass is Jewish.

My first doubt was sewn.

My second arose from dimly wondering why a vampire would even hang out in a cemetery. Yes, they have to sleep somewhere. But everything I had read and seen on the subject during an adolescence fascinated by horror novels and movies suggested vampires were more at home ... at home. In castles and mansions, places where they could surround themselves with all the creature comforts of the afterlife, entertain guests, kick back and relax. Who among them would ever want to spend his time in a damp, dark graveyard?

And my third doubt? Well, that was planted by the very source of the information we were working from, the elder brother of a friend who, to put it politely, had always been a fang or two short of a mouthful of teeth.

He was not a bad person. It was he, after all, who owned the Super 8 projector upon which, in those dark days before VHS and DVD, we watched so many great movies, projected onto a roll-up screen that seemed enormous compared to the TVs of the day and soundtracked in deafening monophonic.

He favored the Hammer studio's output, and I readily admit that my own ongoing fascination with that genre is wholly down to him. And he was a bit of a moviemaker himself, inasmuch as he could spin out stories that, had they appeared on film, would have been utterly spellbinding blockbusters.

Such as The Great Vampire Hunt of March 1970.

In February 1970, occultist Seán Manchester was largely indistinguishable from any of the melee of young people who claimed, while visiting Highgate Cemetery at night in search of the graveyard's already well-documented host of hauntings, that they had seen "a ghost." So many people had a story to tell, and so many stories were told, that one does not even feel blasé summing them up as a run-of-the-mill panoply of spectral cyclists, gray ladies, and headless coachmen.

Manchester, however, was original. No Victorian wraith or chain-entombed specters for him. His sighting, he told the local newspaper, was a "King Vampire of the Undead," and he had a convincing backstory to support his supposition: how in the early eighteenth century, the remains of a highborn Wallachian necromancer had been transported to London by sundry followers and installed in a crypt in the cemetery. Around a century before the cemetery itself existed, but no matter.

Why we don't know, but that doesn't really matter. Even the best-attested folklore is scarcely rich with explanatory minutiae, and besides, who needs facts and figures when we have nobles and necromancers? Certainly not the unnamed coven of modern-day Satanists, who, it was said, conspired to awaken the gent from his eternal slumbers and unleash him in all his vampiric fury upon the cemetery's dark and winding pathways.

I bought a book. I still have it today, and inasmuch as everything I knew about Satanism and the occult was drawn from its pages, it is safe to say that *Devil Worship in Britain* by A. V. Sellwood and Peter Haining remains among the most influential books I have ever read. But though its pages are replete with animal sacrifice, church desecrations, graveyard exhumations, and curses galore, Highgate did not receive a mention.

Instead, old newspaper articles told the story.

At the end of February 1970, the local *Hampstead and Highgate Express* interviewed Manchester, and the headline left little to the imagination. "Does a Vampyr walk in Highgate?" it demanded, and the answer appeared to be an unequivocal yes.

Because other people came forward with their own sightings. Another occult leader, David Farrant, claimed to have discovered the possibly exsanguinated corpses of several foxes lying in the

5

cemetery. Other reports, dating back as far as 1960, told of dogs found in a similar state.

And two weeks after that initial interview, on Friday, March 13 (of course), local television interviews with both Farrant and Manchester led to a crowd that was estimated at two-hundred-plus descending upon the cemetery, swarming over its fences, walls, and locked gates, and...

...and nothing. They did some roaming and running and shouting; an idiot few sadly committed some vandalism. But no vampire was found, no corpses were staked, and the media moved away.

But did the vampire? Or his persecutors? A few months later, on Lammas Day (August 1), the headless, burned remains of a woman missing since the March vampire hunt were discovered in the cemetery grounds. According to some reports, the body had been completely drained of blood, and the head was never found. Police suspected Satanists—or at least, a killer who wanted to pass as one—but more susceptible souls added this victim to the list of vampire kills. And to the best of my knowledge, the perpetrator(s) of the original crime were never identified.

Meanwhile, both Farrant and Manchester continued visiting the cemetery, both by day and surreptitiously at night, and their later (1980s and beyond) writings gaudily document the successes and otherwise that they met with on their hunts. In truth, however, the whole thing was forgotten until Farrant himself was arrested and jailed in 1974, charged with vandalism and desecration within the cemetery. The Highgate Vampire was news again. So we, my vampire-slaying friends and I, struck out to stake it once and for all.

We arrived just in time to see the gates being locked for the night, briefly considered breaking in and taking our chances with any patrolling security, then went home. Vampire hunting makes more sense during the daylight hours, anyway. Our prey would put up less of a fight.

This may be why, with the exception of Buffy, vampire slayers are seldom accorded the same respect and admiration that clings to the vampires themselves. Nobody lining up to watch the latest adventures of Dracula did so through an unerring devotion to Van Helsing, and few people watching the deathless count dispatching his latest attacker ever feels any lasting remorse for the death of the hapless hunter.

The death of a vampire, however—that elicits a very different response.

There is a sense of loss, regret that something so old and beautiful should have so peremptorily been put to the sword without any regard or respect for all the centuries that unfolded prior to its final moments. The death of a vampire, in those terms, can be compared to the destruction of a fine old building, and if the destruction is deliberate, then even greater shame should be heaped upon the shoulders of those responsible.

There is also betrayal, disbelief that immortality can be snuffed out to suddenly. What does that say for those religious beliefs that also promise everlasting life? Everlasting until … what? And that is not a slash at Christianity; or if it is, it is one that is as old as the vampire legend itself. Among the manifold "signs" that the Catholic Church requires before a person can be elevated to sainthood, the incorruptibility of the body, for years after its interment, has always been regarded as a very significant one. But saints are not the only people whose postmortem slumbers are left uninterrupted by decay. Vampires sleep just as soundly.

In fact, that is one of the few pieces of accepted vampire lore that *True Blood* has not driven its own stake through the heart of. Because it has certainly dismissed a lot of the other things that two centuries of popular entertainment have led us to believe will protect us from, or at least alert us to, a passing vampire. The bloodsuckers' off-hand treatment of mirrors, crosses, garlic, and holy water is one of the series' most important contributions to vampire lore in general—especially when aligned to the suggestion that vampires themselves invented most of these legends as a means of ensuring they could continue to move unnoticed.

They don't burst into flames when the sunlight hits them either ("Well, not immediately," quipped Vampire Bill Compton, a few episodes before being done to a crisp by a walk in the park), although you can understand why that fate will never truly be dispensed with. Think of all the SFX creators with a nice line in charbroiling who would suddenly find themselves out of work.

With all this (and more) in mind, this book is *not* dedicated to the fine art of seeking out contradictions in vampire lore. It would be an exaggeration to state that every fresh treatment of the vampire mythos brings its own peculiarities to bear on the basics of vampirology, but a lot of them do, and somewhere, no doubt, there is a website or a thesis that evaluates and compares every one of them.

Neither is this book an attempt to discover why we are so fascinated by our bloodsucking brethren—which, in turn, feeds our insatiable appetite for the tales of Sookie Stackhouse. We should simply accept that we are. Of all the myriad heroes, villains, and all-purpose protagonists who haunt the halls of popular culture, not one even comes close to the ubiquity of the vampire. And it is the manifestations of that fascination that I am concerned with here: the fact that you could stock the average small-town library with every book and magazine article ever to reference vampires and still have plenty left over to store in the annex; the fact that a lifetime could be spent watching vampire movies and TV, and old age would claim you before you reached the end.

Watched in one long, feverish sitting, without breaking to eat, sleep, or pee, *True Blood* alone, as of this writing, would devour three days straight; *Buffy* would consume another week. You could spend another day watching Christopher Lee's *Dracula* flicks, and almost as long devouring the *Underworld* saga. Yet one doubts whether anybody reading this would balk at doing so, if they only had the opportunity—and the stamina.

Why? Because vampire entertainment is almost as compulsive as the vampire itself. Almost as irresistible and, ultimately, almost as enduring. People have been reading, writing, and conjuring fictional vampires for over two centuries. They have been talking about them for even longer. With the obvious exception of ghosts, and the possible addition of were-creatures (if we expand their definition to include any creature that can change its form into that of a human when it feels the need), mankind's love affair with vampires is the oldest that it has. And if we believe what we were told in an old *Doctor Who* (see chapter 1), they're going to last a lot longer as well.

Not that vampires are all we are concerned with here. *True Blood*, after all, has introduced a veritable panoply of supernatural beings and beasties into our world, from the maenad Maryann Forrester, with her dastardly scheme to sacrifice the shape shifter Sam to the god Dionysus; to the Wiccan coven leader Marnie Stonebrook, whose necromantic skills so alarm the vamps; from voodoo witch doctors to fairy mind readers; from V-crazed werewolves to…you've read the books, you've seen the show. There is no need for me to go on.

We also join *True Blood* in celebrating the demise of the sometimes one-dimensional bloodsuckers we encounter in other fiction. Through Sookie, we have met the neo-Nazi Russell Edgington, a twenty-eight-hundred-year-old Celt who barks German when he gets annoyed; Eric, a nightclub-owning Viking warrior; the Romanov Prince Alexei; the aforementioned Elvis Presley…. Here, too, we will encounter a wealth of characters, a wealth of creatures, a world that has slipped beyond the shadows of our own to populate itself with some of humanity's oldest and most powerful nightmares—and/or fantasies.

So switch off your favorite TV show for a while, and put the novels back on the shelf. Sookie will still be there when you return. And instead, relax into a whole other world of gothic grimness, vampiric vivacity, and just occasionally, supernatural silliness. Because if you like *True Blood*, you're going to love…

A classic beauty. *The Vampire* (1897), by artist Philip Burne-Jones.
(Author's collection)

1

VAMPS IN TIME AND SPACE:
THE ARCHAEOLOGY OF FEAR

Tales of the supernatural are as old as storytelling itself, regardless of how they are regarded today. To an alien, arriving on Earth with no understanding of what might pass as religion, the parables of a vengeful god turning women to salt and reducing cities to ashes, demanding sacrifice and devising gruesome tests of fidelity, would appear as horrific as any latter-day slasher film—more so, in fact, for at least the slasher is nominally human. The idea of a vast, all-powerful, all-knowing, but completely invisible consciousness, toying and tormenting its minions simply because it can, is truly the stuff of nightmares.

Grimm's fairy tales are laden with incidents that, were we to discover them in adulthood (rather than devour them as infants), run the gamut from sexual titillation to heart-stopping terror, and often hand in hand. Director Neil Jordan's film treatment of the story of Little Red Riding Hood, 1984's *The Company of Wolves*, is simply the best modern stab at lifting that particular sheet. But it is by no means the only one.

Werewolves were alive and well in ancient Greek and Rome—Plato is one of several sources for the tale of the Arcadian King Lycaon, stricken with lycanthropy as a divine punishment for sacrificing his own son. Even Frankenstein's creature, the most "modern" of the so-called classic monsters, surely forged from the fears aroused by the concurrent French and Industrial Revolutions, has his prehistoric antecedents, as the subtitle to Mary Godwin's original saga makes plain. "The Modern Prometheus" indeed.

Ghost stories, too, have an ancient pedigree. Classical authors Horace and Perseus people their works with the returning dead, historians Herodotus and Tacitus record the appearance of fearful apparitions, and Old and New Testaments alike have their share of phantoms. Pliny even couches his ghost in clanking, rattling chains, some sixteen centuries before a similarly garbed Jacob Marley dropped by to enliven Scrooge's Christmas Eve. The parodist Lucian, too, got in on the act, not only proving that the Roman Empire firmly believed in ghosts, but that the belief was sufficiently entrenched to have bred a race of nonbelievers, too.

Shakespeare, of course, was lousy with the things.

Despite such traditions, horror (as opposed to ghost) stories as we recognize them today have still to celebrate their second centennial. Written in 1816 (and published two years later), Mary Godwin's *Frankenstein* is generally regarded as the first modern horror story, and its influence upon the literary world of the age simply cannot be quantified. By the end of the decade, horror writing was exercising some of the greatest—and the crassest—writing minds of the age, fermenting a school of endeavor that, over the next eighty years, would see the Victorian pen perceive nightmares that still haunt our hearts today: Bram Stoker's *Dracula*, Robert Louis Stevenson's *Dr. Jekyll and Mr. Hyde*, Harrison Ainsworth's *The Lancashire Witches*, and so on and so forth.

Neither is it coincidence that these tales, or variations thereon, remain the bedrock of horror today. Whether a modern audience's tastes lean toward the more sophisticated end of things or are happiest sloshing about in kitsch and ketchup, there is little under the sun that is new, and when the sun has set and darkness falls, there is little under the moon that's new either.

DOCTOR WHO AND THE VAMPIRES

But here's a thought: What if vampires, as opposed to being a separate species from mankind—which most bloodsuckers seem to believe they are—were actually its ultimate destination? The final form of evolution before the entire planet decays itself into pollution-powered extinction?

That is the underlying proposal beneath *The Curse of Fenric*, a 1989 story within the long-running BBC TV series *Doctor Who*. And it's a good one. The Haemovores are vastly powerful, telepathic creatures whose taste for blood appears to have been born out of the absence of any other edible foodstuffs in a future world that has been wiped clear of nourishment by industrial fumes and chemical sludge. They have taken, too, to living beneath the sea; the land itself is poisonous to the touch.

There they would have remained, feeding on the last of a dwindling stock of unevolved humans and themselves spiraling into extinction, had one of their number, the so-called Ancient One, not been snatched back into the planet's history by a time storm. He emerges into ninth-century Transylvania, from whence he begins the entire cycle anew, creating fresh Haemovores by passing along the genetic infection that is the defining characteristic of his race. And it is their offspring who became the vampires of our own myth and legend.

Yet the Haemovores, with what was then (but is sadly no longer) the show's traditional taste for guile, were not the focal point of the ensuing adventure. Rather, they were merely the foot soldiers of a far greater menace: an elemental force of evil, as old as the universe itself, who went by the name of Fenric. It is he whom the titular Doctor battles, with the Ancient One an unlikely ally who wishes only to be returned to his own time.

It's an intriguing premise, and one that the confirmed *Who* addict wishes had been expanded upon. But no matter, because the Ancient One and his cronies were not the only vamps stalking what acolytes refer to as the Whoniverse.

There is also the menace of the Saturnyns, a race that bears an unfortunate resemblance to an especially creative night at the local surf 'n' turf emporium. With their lobster claws, fishy heads, and vaguely mammalian torsos, the Saturnyns also had designs on the planet Earth, transforming it into a vast colony of their home planet by disguising themselves as attractive young women and draining the blood of whomever fell into their clutches. The Doctor encounters them in 1580 in Venice (hence the episode title "The Vampires of Venice," broadcast in 2010), and confirms the race's historical right to claim the vampiric mantle with the discovery that the Saturnyns are combustibly susceptible to large doses of ultraviolet light.

But if we want to go back to the very beginning, then the Great Vampire is where any self-respecting *Doctor Who* fan will direct us— to a story, "State of Decay," transmitted in 1980 (but originally commissioned three years earlier, when it was placed on hold for fears that it might overload an audience already thrilling to the BBC's latest adaptation of *Dracula*).

The Great Vampire is another of the elemental forces of the universe, a race of creatures that emerged during the dark days of chaos that preceded the birth of the universe as we know it, and whose appetite was so voracious that they could as easily drain the life force from an entire planet as they could suck a single human being dry.

As vampires go, they don't get much tougher than that. Or much older. Yet there is also something strangely unsatisfying about each of these "solutions": a sense that the vampire as we know and love it should not, and will not, be written off as either a mutation or a space invader. For to do so negates one of the principle characteristics of the breed that we find most fascinating: the vampire's complete and absolute absence of humanity, but simultaneously, the lengths to which one will travel in order to persuade a potential victim that it has some.

Would the Ancient One have fallen in love with Sookie?

Would a Saturnyn have wined and dined Mina Harker?

Would the Great Vampire have ever opened an antiques store in Jerusalem's Lot?

Doctor Who's vampires, in cahoots with so many other science fiction–derived beings, utilize brute strength and hunger alone. A true vampire employs those talents only when there is no call, or need, for any other.

STALKING THE CENTURIES: VAMPIRE LEGEND IN ANCIENT DAYS

Set out to unearth the history of vampirism, and you will swiftly discover that the myths and legends of ancient Rome, Greece, and Mesopotamia all flirt with vampiric lore. So do the cultures of the ancient Indus Valley, modern Nepal, Tibet, and India. In fact, most of the races whose long-ago lives form the very DNA of modern civilization had, somewhere in their belief system, a fear of the nocturnal bloodsucker.

In Greek mythology, Empousa was the beautiful, flame-haired daughter of the goddess Hecate and a ghoul named Mormo—a fiend, insisted parents of the day, who was characterized by an alarmingly disciplinarian penchant for biting misbehaving children. Empousa, on the other hand, favored young men, slipping in while they were sleeping and draining their bodies of blood before savagely devouring the flesh. A vampire with attitude!

Although she was originally termed a demigoddess, Empousa's high stature did not linger, at least outside of her own cult. Indeed, by the time the playwright Aristophanes came to compose his *Ecclesiazusae* (*The Assembly Women*, or *Women in Parliament*) during the fourth century BC, she had already been transformed into "some weird beast…some big blister full of blood and ugly gore," a reference that certain translations have rephrased as "some sort of vampire." Today she is most often aligned with sundry other flesh-and-blood-devouring denizens of the netherworld, the *lamia*, for example, and the *Laistrygones*—the cannibalistic giants who accounted for much of Odysseus's fleet in Homer's *The Odyssey*. Which seems a little cruel bearing in mind her distinguished heritage, but hey, she is scarcely alone in that fate.

Moving on in time, Imperial Rome believed that owls possessed vampiric tendencies, and their modus operandi also sounds familiar; Ovid's *Fasti* cautions of the *strix*, who "fly by night and attack nurseless children and defile them, their throats gorging with blood." The best defense against these nocturnal visitors, apparently, was running water.

In faraway East Asia, the Malay *langsuir* was a beautiful woman with a taste for babies' blood, and the *penanggalen* was a disembodied head that trailed intestines and ate children. The Arab *ghoul* was a female demon who wandered nocturnal cemeteries and drank the blood of the recently dead, and the Chinese *xiang shi* was a corpse that protected itself from death and decay by consuming the blood of both the living and the dead.

The Catholic Church, too, had a strong belief in vampires. The Fourth Lateran Council of 1215 is often said to have acknowledged their existence, although a strict translation of the document appears to be more a general nod toward all manner of supernatural malfeasance: "Diabolus enim et alii daemones a Deo quidem natura creati sunt boni, sed ipsi per se facti sunt mali" (The Devil and the other demons were created by God good in their nature, but they by themselves have made themselves evil).

However, the same document did establish the Church as the only power on Earth strong enough to combat such visitants, and when plague swept fourteenth-century Europe in the guise of the Black Death, vampires were believed to rank among its principal causes, the dead infecting the dead by feeding upon them. A few centuries later, postcolonial New England attributed consumption, or tuberculosis as we now so unimaginatively term it, to a similar cause.

And what was the remedy for any creature considered responsible for these dread visitations? A stake through the heart, and then either beheading or burning. That'll show them who's boss.

HOW TO KILL A VAMPIRE

1. **A Stake Through the Heart:** Although it didn't work in Hammer's *Dracula Has Risen from the Grave* (1968), and different parts of the world preferred different methods, and even different body parts. In Serbia the chosen wood was hawthorn; in Russia it was ash. In parts of Germany, the stake should enter through the vampire's mouth; in Serbia again, the stomach was the chosen target.

2. **Fire:** Although it didn't seem to bother Lestat that much, and both Bill Compton and his maker Lorena survived it without so much as a lingering singe.

3. **Sunlight:** Unless you happen to be hanging with the cast of *The Hunger*, who are happily abroad during the day.

4. **Garlic:** Surprisingly ineffective.

5. **Infected Blood:** *True Blood* toys with a new strain of hepatitis, D, which is harmless to humans but can weaken a vampire. Aside from that, it doesn't really seem to matter.

6. **Silver:** *True Blood* again notwithstanding, silver would appear to be more effective against werewolves than vampires, with its deployment against the lycan in *Underworld* probably standing as the definitive statement.

7. **The Cross, Holy Water, and Assorted Other Religious Paraphernalia:** I hate to keep harping on about that scene in *The Fearless Vampire Killers*, but it does make a very valid point. However, all remain proof against the Hammer movie studio's vampires, with 1973's *The Satanic Rites of Dracula* adding a hawthorn bush to the litany of vampiric allergies, that being the traditional source of Jesus's crown of thorns.

8. **Decapitation:** Archaeology suggests that this was an effective (or, at least, favored) remedy in Balkan folklore, although with legends of the English-speaking world so replete with the tales of headless ghosts (not to mention the supernatural denizen of Sleepy Hollow), one wonders whether this doesn't simply replace one menace with another.

9. **Lemon:** Suspected vampires in Saxony, southern Germany, were buried with a citrus fruit in the mouth; Romanians preferred garlic (see above); medieval Venetians wedged a brick between the suspect's jaws; and the Romany people advocated steel.

10. **Body Piercing:** A number of European cultures recommended embedding sharp objects ranging from scythe blades to needles into the body of any suspected vampire.

Few, if any, of these early vampiric beings accord with what we today "know" to be the race's most defining characteristics. More directly recognizable vampires would emerge over time, however, generally in tandem with the spread of Christianity through Eastern Europe during the Dark Ages and into medieval times. But it would be the early eighteenth century before fear of vampires truly stepped out of Balkan peasant folklore and into Western sensibilities.

In 1718, Austrian officials taking control of the Serbian territories granted to their nation by the Treaty of Passarowitz commenced the task of recording all the local superstitions they had inherited. And one of the most bizarre, they reported, was that of demanding the exhumation of certain bodies to ensure that they were truly dead, and not prone to rising in search of a midnight snack.

Neither did this appear to be an idle fear. A little over a decade later, two Austrian military doctors, Glaser and Flückinger, were dispatched to investigate reports of a vampire plague afflicting a small village called Meduegna. No less than twenty people had been killed by the vampire, whom the locals believed was a recently deceased outlaw named Arnold Paole, who himself had suffered an encounter with a vampire a few years earlier.

On that occasion, Paole claimed, he cured himself of vampirism by eating soil from his tormentor's grave, but perhaps the remedy was not as efficacious as he believed. For no sooner had the hapless Paole passed away, breaking his neck in a fall from a hay wagon, than his vampire form was seen around the village, killing four people before his body was exhumed and staked.

That was in 1726. Five years on, Paole had apparently returned, and two years later, the case was among those that Austrian writer John Heinrich Zopfius compiled into his *Dissertatio de Uampiris Seruiensibus*, or *A Dissertation on Serbian Vampires* (Halle, 1733), the first Western examination of the vampire belief. Vampires, he declared, "issue forth from their graves in the night, attack people sleeping quietly in their beds, suck out all their blood from their bodies and destroy them." And unlike Empousa, the *langsuir*, or any other ancient bogey, "they beset men, women and children alike, sparing neither age nor sex."

There was no doubt, either, about having been attacked. "Those who are under the fatal malignity of their influence complain of suffocation and a total deficiency of spirits, after which they soon expire. Some who, when at the point of death, have been asked if they can tell what is causing their decease, reply that such and such persons, lately dead, have arisen from the tomb to torment and torture them."

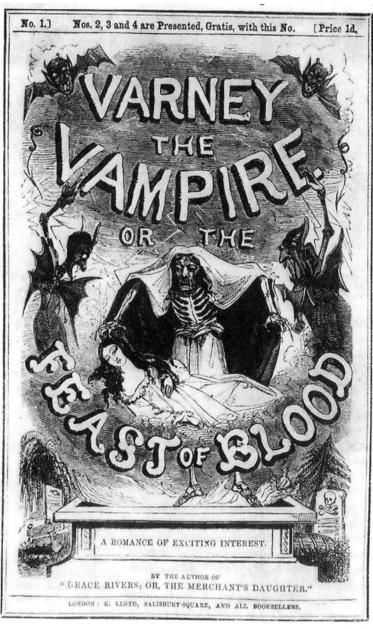

VARNEY THE VAMPIRE OR THE FEAST OF BLOOD

A ROMANCE OF EXCITING INTEREST.

BY THE AUTHOR OF
"GRACE RIVERS; OR, THE MERCHANT'S DAUGHTER."

LONDON: E. LLOYD, SALISBURY-SQUARE, AND ALL BOOKSELLERS.

A magazine recounting the adventures of *Varney the Vampire* kept early Victorian
England on bloodsucking tenterhooks from 1845 to 1847, before the full story
was published in book form in 1847, the year of Bram Stoker's birth.
(Author's collection)

2

FRESH BITES: AN ACCOUNT OF ENGLISH LITERATURE'S EARLIEST ENCOUNTERS WITH VAMPIRES

In 1734, the Serbian word *vampir* made its way into the English-speaking world for the first time. It appeared courtesy of academic John Swinton's privately published travelogue *The Travels of Three English Gentlemen*, a slim work that was originally published as a mere pamphlet. Indeed, *The Travels of Three English Gentlemen* might have been lost to posterity had a copy not found its way into the library of the Earl of Oxford, from whence it was scooped up into Samuel Johnson's *Harleian Miscellany* in 1745.

One of those wonderful old-style magazine digests whose every issue abounded with literary curiosities (its full title was *A Collection of Scarce, Curious, and Entertaining Pamphlets and Tracts, as Well in Manuscript as in Print, Found in the Late Earl of Oxford's Library, Interspersed with Historical, Political, and Critical Notes*), the *Harleian Miscellany* broadcast the news to the nation. Vampires are the "bodies of deceased persons, animated by evil spirits, which come out of the grave in the night-time [to] suck the blood of many of the living and thereby destroy them."

It would be a new century, however, before the vampire first stepped into English literature, when a short story titled "Wake Not the Dead" (often attributed to German romance writer Ludwig Tieck) was published. Well translated and widely read at the time, this salutary warning against reviving a recently deceased spouse, no matter how much she is missed, was still percolating in the collective subconscious two decades later. Genevan theologian Dr. John Polidori's *The Vampyre*, however, lifted it to center stage.

THE VAMPYRE (1819)

Polidori was the oft-forgotten fourth member of the infamous literary gathering that brought Lord Byron, Percy Shelley, and his wife-to-be, Mary Wollstonecraft Godwin, together on the banks of Lake Geneva, Switzerland, in 1816.

There they inaugurated a competition to determine who could compose the best ghost story, a task, arguably, that was never completed. Percy Shelley's *Fragment of a Ghost Story* fizzled out very quickly; and neither Mary's tale of the mad Doctor Frankenstein reanimating a corpse through the means of demented genius and electricity alone, nor the unnamed creature that feeds on Byron's luckless Augustus Darvell while visiting a cemetery close to Ephesus, in Turkey, can be considered ghosts.

But for birthing what would become two of the most successful creations in modern literature, we cannot really fault either of them. (Ken Russell's 1986 movie *Gothic* brilliantly retells the story of the competition.)

Byron's tale was left unfinished. But it was published in 1819, under the title *Fragment of a Novel*, as a postscript of sorts to Byron's latest prolusion, *Mazeppa: A Poem*; and immediately Polidori, Byron's doctor and traveling companion, leaped onto its possibilities as the foundation for his novel *The Vampyre*.

Written, Polidori claimed, over "two or three idle mornings," *The Vampyre* takes its inspiration from Byron's creature, not from his plot. A wealthy young gent named Aubrey is touring Greece when he meets, and falls in love with, the innkeeper's daughter Ianthe. Enter Lord Ruthven, an acquaintance of Aubrey's from London, arriving coincidentally just a few days after Ianthe held Aubrey spellbound with her tales of the local belief in vampires— and just a few days before one of those dread creatures ruthlessly kills her.

Aubrey and Ruthven travel on alone, when they are attacked by brigands. Ruthven is killed in the ensuing melee, but with his dying breath he swears Aubrey to secrecy. Nobody must know he is dead—a peculiar request that is explained only when Aubrey returns to London and discovers Ruthven alive and well, and seducing Aubrey's own sister. Who is discovered dead, drained of all blood, on her wedding night. Of Ruthven, there is no trace.

It's a great tale, written with all the attention to detail that was a hallmark of the literature of the age, and if that makes it feel a little clunky to the modern reader, then who is really at fault for that? It was a massive success at the time, and its enduring popularity would soon give birth to one of the all-time greatest vampire serials: the rip-roaring adventures of Varney the Vampire, published in 109 weekly parts (totaling over half a million words) between 1845 and 1847. Each issue cost a penny; and every one, according to the serious readers and reviewers of the time, was dreadful. A new literary genre was born.

VARNEY THE VAMPIRE (1845) AND THE PENNY DREADFUL

The first penny dreadfuls hit newsstands in the mid-1840s, direct descendants of the serialized novels of Charles Dickens, (William) Harrison Ainsworth, and all those other solid souls whose latest novels appeared initially in monthly magazine form. Yet no matter what base instincts those authors appealed to (and in his early years, even Dickens was condemned for pandering to the lowest common denominator), the dreadfuls were worse, with the best of them delighting in a savagery that the average sensitive reader often found difficult to comprehend.

Reveling in graphic tales of sensationalism and gore, many dreadfuls took their lead from mainstream literature. Such early heroes as the serial prison-breaker Jack Sheppard and the highwayman Dick Turpin had both been immortalized in novel form by Ainsworth, for example, while Varney the Vampire took his name, and at least a soupçon of his personal attributes, from *Lucretia, or The Children of the Night*, the brilliantly titled and breathtakingly thrilling novel by the author Edward Bulwer-Lytton—or the Right Honorable Lord Lytton, as he was known in political and aristocratic circles.

Bulwer-Lytton is a must read for anyone intrigued by Victorian literature, and by fans of classic cliché too. It was he who coined the phrase "the great unwashed" as a nomenclature for the working class; it was he who first suggested that "the pen is mightier than the sword," and best of all, he who coined that most immortal of literary opening sentences, "It was a dark and stormy night." How could he fail?

Lucretia, despite both the resonance of its title and the insinuations of its subtitle, is not a vampire story. Bulwer-Lytton claimed the story was written to illustrate "the darker side of human nature," a task that it amply fulfilled, while inspiration for the saga's hero, Gabriel Varney, was drawn from the misdeeds of Thomas Wainewright, a respected author and artist turned forger and poisoner, whose story had already inspired Charles Dickens's *Martin Chuzzlewit*. Indeed, Bulwer-Lytton acknowledged that his novel was motivated by the interest awakened in Wainewright's case both by Dickens and another celebrated case of poisoning, committed by one Tawell the Quaker. Whereas Dickens drove toward some fine morality and upstanding resolutions, however, Bulwer-Lytton went for the jugular.

Wainewright is portrayed as Gabriel Varney; his sister-in-law as Helen Mainwaring; his wife (who was implicated, but never charged, in the murder) as Varney's stepmother, Lucretia. And it is she who takes center stage in the tale, a winding labyrinth in which the secret poisons of the Borgias (hence, of course, the name of the novel's heroine) have been revealed to Varney's father, to be deployed by the wicked Lucretia.

Thus it is Lucretia, not Varney, whose misdeeds map out the story. But the name was clearly an evocative one, at least to author James Malcolm Rymer (or perhaps to Thomas Preskett Prest; the story's parentage has never been truly ascertained). Unapologetically he lifted it for the hero of his own tale, and *Varney the Vampire* would emerge as one of the most gripping sagas of the age—and one of the most influential too.

The tale is not necessarily cohesive. Perhaps as a consequence of its episodic nature, the story keeps only the lightest of eyes on continuity, and reading it in one solid burst (it was published in book form in 1847 and is still readily available today), one does occasionally grow bewildered as time and place slip around according only to the most recent vagaries of the plot.

It is unclear how Varney even became a vampire. In one chapter, he claims to have been cursed by a Royalist after betraying his whereabouts to a Commonwealth soldier during the English Civil War; in another, he was the victim of a Frankensteinian experiment, hanged for crimes committed in life and then revived by a mad medical student who was experimenting with electricity. As for the vampirism itself, we must remember that the genre was still young at the time, at least in literary terms, and its authors were very much making things up as they went along. Varney feeds on blood, but he can also eat and drink human food (although he does not especially enjoy it). He has no aversion to sunlight, garlic, or crucifixes, but he is astonishingly powerful—a skilled hypnotist— and in his most lasting legacy, when he feeds, his fangs leave two puncture wounds in the throat of his victim.

> *Her bosom heaves and her limbs tremble, yet she cannot withdraw her eyes from the marble-looking face.*

And later,

> *With a plunge he seizes her neck in his fang-like teeth, a gush of blood and hideous sucking noise follows. The girl has swooned and the vampire is at his hideous repast.*

In terms of a story that never lets up, that never (well, rarely) allows itself to sink into scene-setting sludgery, and that paints no greater portraits of its protagonists than are strictly necessary for them to be dispatched with gory glory, *Varney the Vampire* is probably the greatest of all nineteenth-century vampire tales. It certainly outstrips *The Vampyre*, it easily out-gruesomes *Carmilla* (see chapter 4), and it's a lot more dramatic than *Dracula*—which, for all its subsequent fame and influence, is actually a lot less enjoyable to read than it is to contemplate in the light of its subsequent rewrites, revisions, and re-creations.

Bram Stoker is unquestionably the father of the modern vampire story, and *Dracula* is the seed with which he impregnated popular culture. But it is Varney, with his endless ambition, ruthless cruelty, guileless charm, and heartless romance, who truly stands at the apex of modern vampdom. And he wasn't an impaler, either.

GOOD LADY DUCAYNE (1896)

Fifty years elapsed between the publication of *Varney the Vampire* and the literary reemergence of his kinsfolk—half a century during which the vampire maintained only a marginal hold on the imagination of the English reading public. A short story, German author Karl von Wachsmann's "The Mysterious Stranger," appeared in *Chambers Repository* magazine in 1854 (it was published in Germany a decade earlier), and so impressed the young writer M. R. James (later renowned for his ghost stories) that he still remembered it seventy years later.

In 1896, however, one of Victorian England's most prolific romance novelists, the now sixty-year-old Mary Elizabeth Braddon, gifted readers of *The Strand* magazine with *Good Lady Ducayne*, a story that utterly reignited the vampiric fascination and rightfully so. It is an excellent romp, tracking the fiendish machinations of the titular Milady in an age (literarily if not culturally) when it was polite to regard as mere unfortunate coincidence that two successive companions of a much-respected aristocrat had passed away within weeks of arriving in her service.

> *"They were poor, feeble creatures," Francine told [Bella]. "They looked fresh and bright enough when they came to Miladi; but they ate too much and they were lazy. They died of luxury and idleness. Miladi was too kind to them. They had nothing to do; and so they took to fancying things; fancying the air didn't suit them, that they couldn't sleep."*

The fact that the story is now all but forgotten, and certainly lost beneath the weight of the much-published Braddon's other works, is one of those inexplicable tragedies with which literature abounds. But the vampire, having been aroused, was not about to go the same way.

BRAM STOKER AND *DRACULA* (1897)

Bram Stoker, the business manager at the Lyceum Theatre on London's Strand, was one of those who had never lost the faith. Born in 1847—that is, the same year as *Varney* was first published in book form—he had devoured that story as a child, and made no secret of the fact that its influence had awakened further curiosities.

Even into his forties, the bookish Stoker avidly devoured folk tales and mythologies emanating from the vampire's "traditional" homelands in Eastern Europe, while Sheridan Le Fanu's provocative *Carmilla* was seldom far from his bedside following its publication in 1872. A place, it might be noted, that was not necessarily derived wholly from its vampiric content. We will be visiting with *Carmilla* later in this book … in, perhaps, an even more appropriate setting than the confines of the Stoker boudoir. Suffice, for now, to say that if there was one aspect of the future vampire that *Varney* forgot to dwell on and Braddon was perhaps too polite to embrace, it was naked eroticism—a quality that *Carmilla* oozed from every paragraph.

Dracula's other forebears ranged far and wide. M. R. James cited the aforementioned "The Mysterious Stranger" as a direct ancestor of Stoker's tale. It is also common knowledge that the count's very name came from Vlad III "the Impaler," a cruel and ruthless fifteenth-century king of Wallachia whose nickname came from his favored method of execution, and whose victims reportedly numbered in the tens of thousands. *Dracul*, which translates from Romanian as "the Dragon," was a title conferred in 1431 upon his father, Vlad II, in the form of the honorary Order of the Dragon. Vlad III then inherited the title in the form *Dracula*, which means "Son of the Dragon." And so literature's most infamous vampire took his name from a real-life historical monster.

Familiar is the revelation that the sweeping extravagance of Dracula's mannerisms, most commonly draped in a smoothly flowing cloak, was based on those exhibited by the actor Henry

Irving, Stoker's boss at the Lyceum; and finally, that perhaps the best-known elements of the tale—its title and its hero's name—were both very much last-minute additions. Through many of its earliest drafts, the novel was titled *The Dead Un-Dead*, and told the story of Count Wampyr. And perhaps there is an alternate universe in which those original plans remain unchanged. One wonders whether the book is as legendary there as it is in our reality.

Stoker's own experiences also shaped the story.

In August 1888, the Lyceum was rejoicing in one of the most successful stage plays of the season, an imported American adaptation of Robert Louis Stevenson's *The Strange Case of Dr. Jekyll and Mr. Hyde*. The tale of a mild-mannered physician who, by quaffing a potion of his own invention, is transformed into a malevolent, murdering monster, *Jekyll and Hyde* created a sensation from the moment it opened on August 4. But it was not the gripping presentation alone that attracted attention. The sickening realism of the murder scenes, too, grasped the headlines, first in the review sections and then on the front pages after the goriest of them came brutally to life. Less than a month after the play opened, London awoke to news of the first of the five vicious slaughters that criminal history now attributes to Jack the Ripper.

Immediately, actor Richard Mansfield, so convincing in the Lyceum play's title role(s), found himself among the very first characters to come under suspicion for the actual killings. Then, when his innocence was established to all, the play itself came under the spotlight for possibly inspiring the killer in the first place.

Like a whodunit with the final chapter torn out, the Ripper was never apprehended. Some 125 years after the fact, he has not even been identified. But his reign of terror, brief though it appears by modern standards (just ten weeks from start to finish), continues to stalk the international psyche, not only for the sake of the mystery, but also because of the unparalleled brutality of the executions.

In choosing to transplant his Transylvanian count to the same mean East London streets as had been so recently haunted by the Ripper, Bram Stoker ruthlessly (and, one presumes, deliberately) rekindled fears that had never been laid to rest. Namely, the fact that the killer remained at liberty. Indeed, those souls who blamed the Rippings themselves on some unknown supernatural entity could have taken no comfort whatsoever from the knowledge that the city was again under attack from a being whose bloodlust knew no limits.

With so much sensationalism in its favor, the book was very well received, at least among the critics of the age. Its actual sales were low, but Stoker's friend Sir Arthur Conan Doyle described *Dracula* as "the very best story of diablerie which I have read for many years," while the *Daily Mail* newspaper compared it to *Frankenstein* and Edgar Allan Poe's *The Fall of the House of Usher* before concluding: "*Dracula* is even more appalling in its gloomy fascination than any one of these." But the highest accolade was still to come, as the most fervent admirers of all hoisted Stoker to the very pinnacle of the gothic school of literature, to stand alongside the undisputed queen of that territory, Ann Radcliffe.

An engraved scene (by David Henry Friston) from Sheridan Le Fanu's sapphic
masterpiece, *Carmilla* (1872). (Author's collection)

3

A LITTLE GOTHIC INTERLUDE

We are going to be hearing a lot more about it as this book rolls on, so let's get it out of the way right now. Gothic is irrational. It is inhuman, it is hopeless. It is the knowledge that mankind is puny, its dreams, loves, and achievements barely amounting to even atoms in the face of fate. Only one human emotion holds itself erect before the enormity of all that is laid out before, below, above, and around it; only one emotion is timeless, deathless, and endless. Fear.

Gothic is fear—the desolation and hopelessness that hold sway no matter what mankind does to crush them, the ineffable sense of self-worthlessness that dresses in black when the world is in color, that waits for death while life is in full bloom, that prides beauty over rationality, but prizes ugliness higher than even that.

The 1990s fascination with body piercing was no more an affectation than the absinthe-quaffing wastrels of the age of Byron, or the swooning damsels of Mrs. Radcliffe, sipping cumulatively lethal doses of belladonna in order to achieve the dilated pupils of beautiful fashion—and whose legacy lives on in the exaggerated panda eyes of modern gothic-chick glamour.

Gothic is self-perpetuating. When Ian Curtis, singer with the band Joy Division, was found hanging in his kitchen, Iggy Pop's *The Idiot* LP was spinning on the turntable. Neither Joy Division nor Iggy were goths, but their music was certainly goth*ic*, beholden to an aesthetic that is as old as man and as black as his heart.

But most of all, gothic is the art of performance, the ultimate artifice in and through which we might discover the ultimate reality. For what, after all, is fantasy if not the direct embodiment of our deepest dreams? And what are dreams if not the shrouded land where gothic is all there is?

At least that's one way of looking at it.

Because you could also agree that gothic style in its purest state is deplorably dull, a featureless plain of atmosphere, imagery, and silence. For that reason, and that reason alone, great gothic, genuine gothic, has always been accompanied by so much more than its own gothic elements. Humor is a part of it. So is violence, so is sexuality and most potently of all, so is schlock.

Few readers in the late eighteenth century ever described the novels of Horace Walpole as instant "classics," but today, *The Castle of Otranto* is regarded among the greatest gothic romances of all time. Similarly, from Mary Godwin to Christopher Lee, *Frankenstein* is most readily pictured not as an allegorical account of mob rule and revolution, but as a sickly green, breezeblock-headed lumbering lump with bolts in its neck. Gothic is sensuous, sensual, and sibilant. But it is also the carnival of cruelty, the theater of shadows, the burlesque of blood.

Gothic is not about intellectualism. It is about aesthetics, and while that in itself raises the genre high above the aspirations of the common herd, which gather gray and unyielding around the totems of modern consumerism, it finds more common ground with camp than cant—or indeed, Kant. Neither is gothic especially concerned with the classicism of the term itself, although archaeology gaily traces its roots back more than four hundred years, and the enterprising scholar is more than welcome to trace the tendrils forward. The parallels can prove richly rewarding.

The work of the seventeenth-century Italian landscape artist Salvator Rosa is seized upon as its starting point as an object of beauty, and none could deny that his best-known images— *Landscape with Cave*, *The Death of Regulus*, *Scene of Witchcraft*— put into pictures the thoughts of the damned. Rosa can also be credited with the invention of gothic as a musical pursuit; although it is generally perceived as a poem, his "La Strega" ("The Witch") was conceived as a musical number, with lyrics that cry out for a modern-rock reinvention. It was intended, surmised Rosa's 1995 biographer Jonathan Scott, to be "sung on a dark evening by a powerful soprano or, perhaps, by a counter-tenor." And under those so favorable circumstances, "it may have tingled the spine."

> *Putrid blood, oozing guts, dried mummies, bones and grubs*
> *Fumigations that will blacken, horrid cries that terrify*

Since Rosa's time, gothic has become a peculiarly English pursuit. Of course, the manifold tangents down which the nation's creative juices flowed during the ensuing centuries often forced it out of the limelight, even back into obscurity. But in literature, poetry, art, theater, even horticulture and architecture, the thread remained—sometimes frayed, sometimes tangled, but never truly broken.

And the thread begins with Mrs. Radcliffe.

MRS. RADCLIFFE

There's a lot of Mrs. Radcliffe in the work of Charlaine Harris. The same attention to detail, the same refusal to be hurried, and the same eye for something nasty creeping just beyond the periphery of vision.

Of course, you could say much the same for a lot of other writers, too. But if a Louisiana shack were an Italianate castle, if a secretive bar owner was a mysterious Duke, and if a shy, prudish waitress became an aristocratic heiress, then the heritage would be unmistakable.

As a style of storytelling, gothic has its roots in those invariably overlong, inevitably overwrought (and so sadly, very seldom read today) volumes published by a select handful of authors across the course of years loosely defined by the literary reigns of Horace Walpole in the mid-eighteenth century and Jane Austen in the early nineteenth. Of these, Ann Radcliffe was, and remains, the greatest.

Storm-blasted moors, creaking gibbets, dilapidated castles, mysterious monks, whispered warnings, cackling madmen, unseen messengers, secret corridors, malevolent guardians, doomed lovers. All of these and more numbered among the standard fixtures and fittings, and although they were drawn from countless archetypes, it was not the already established theatrical melancholy of tradition that appealed. It was its potential for *further* theatricality. Anyone could walk through the ruins of some ancient castle and revel in their stark silence and beautiful decay. Artists painted them, poets contemplated them, architects attempted to duplicate them. It was authors, however, who imposed the silent, gliding figures that sidled up behind these worthies and froze their blood with a sudden sound. *Boo!*

First uttered in print (I am speaking figuratively here) by Horace Walpole, one of the finest "popular" authors of the eighteenth century, it is that *Boo!* that distinguished—perhaps even formulated—gothic literature. But though Walpole was its creator, he was never its master. Indeed, by the end of that same century, he had been eclipsed many times over by Ann (or, as she was better known to earlier generations, simply Mrs.) Radcliffe, a writer who redeployed those same devices with such unerring accuracy that, for the last twenty-five years of her life, many of her readers believed she had already died, her mind hopelessly deranged by the horrors she detailed in her novels. It was an easy mistake to make.

Mrs. Radcliffe's first book, *The Castles of Athlin and Dunbayne: A Highland Story*, was published in 1789; by the time of her fourth, *The Mysteries of Udolpho* in 1794, she was the most popular writer in the Western world, outselling Shakespeare, the Bible, *Pilgrim's Progress*—the lot. It's true: the name under which she chose to write does make her sound like a disapproving schoolteacher, or perhaps a particularly ferocious librarian. It is also true that to generations accustomed to knowing their favorite authors by their full names (or, at best, their full pseudonyms), the idea of impatiently anticipating the latest prolusion of Mrs. Radcliffe seems somewhat less appealing than, say, awaiting the next novel by Charlaine Harris—or for those of such inclination, Stephenie Meyer.

Two centuries ago, however, Mrs. Radcliffe was *the* mistress of all that she surveyed. And she surveyed an awful lot.

Her literary career was short—just five novels published between 1789 and 1797, and a sixth published posthumously in 1826. She was intensely private. A handful of surviving pen pictures describe her as a beautiful woman, but no contemporary portrait of her exists. She made no public appearances, she curried no friendships with the literati of the day. When the poet Christina Rossetti set about writing Radcliffe's biography, she was forced to abandon the project because there was simply nothing to write.

But her stories ...oh, her stories. According to Radcliffe's husband William, himself editor of *The English Chronicle*, she started writing as a means of whiling away the hours when he was forced to work late or travel. She would then read her tales to him when he came home, absorbing him within a universe that was as far as can be imagined from their comfortable home in London: a universe littered with dark and foreboding castles and ruins, peopled by mysterious European noblemen, haunted by breathless heroines, assailed by the supernatural.

Singlehandedly, Mrs. Radcliffe created that vein of gothic romance that still persists today and overhangs every significant author of the next century and more, from Sir Walter Scott, who once proclaimed "her prose was poetry and her poetry was prose," to Jane Austen, whose fictional meeting with Radcliffe in the movie *Becoming Jane* is portrayed as the incident that galvanized Austen toward her own writing career; from Edgar Allan Poe, who adapted so many Radcliffian elements for his own ends, to Daphne du Maurier, whose *Rebecca* is alive with her echoes.

The young Harrison Ainsworth proclaimed his ambition was to tell stories "in the bygone style of Mrs. Radcliffe, substituting an old English squire, an old English manorial residence and an old English highwayman for the Italian marchese, the castle and the brigand of the great mistress of Romance," and when the poet Shelley visited Cuckfield Place, an ancient home in the English county of Sussex, he delightedly declared that it reminded him of "bits of Mrs. Radcliffe."

And then there was Bram Stoker, who essentially housed Dracula in a castle straight out of *The Mysteries of Udolpho*, and worked hard, too, to allow his characters the same breath of consolation—that none of what was happening was actually real—that Mrs. Radcliffe reserved for her heroines. No matter how dark their adventures seemed, how inexplicably macabre and occult, Radcliffe's supernatural was always revealed to have a natural cause in the end. Bram Stoker was not the first of her disciples to make it appear as though that was the case once again and then reverse that solution. But he was the first to make it so obvious that that was his plan.

We do not question today how great Mrs. Radcliffe was. A better question would be: how great could she have been? There she was, at the pinnacle of her profession, with her fifth novel, *The Italian, or The Confessional of the Black Penitents*, emerging as spellbinding as its predecessors; and then—nothing.

Not another tale did she tell, not a word did she write. It was as though the Earth had simply opened up and swallowed her, and of course rumor and intrigue rose to fill the void; what else could they do? Even the rock singer Syd Barrett, surely her closest modern counterpart in terms of genius left hanging on the brink, had the decency to keep his contemporaries at least loosely apprised of his possible whereabouts. Radcliffe simply vanished, and did so so effectively that when she did finally pass away in 1823, felled by pneumonia resulting from a bronchial infection, even some of her old friends were shocked to learn that they had to begin their mourning all over again. They had assumed her dead long before.

Radcliffe's abdication itself, of course, is the stuff of gripping preternatural fiction; indeed, it has been suggested that she personally stage-managed her entire seclusion as a work of art in its own right, that the gossip and rumor that sprang up in her absence was itself the long-awaited final novel. That's as may be. Either way, Radcliffe got out while she was still on top. There are a lot of other artists who could learn from her example.

Few people read Mrs. Radcliffe today. The problem, and this is true of Stoker too, is that the very act of originating a particular genre (or being perceived to have done so; as David Bowie once said, "It doesn't matter who did something first; it's who does it second that counts") will also lead to cliché and redundancy. Other people take the baton and run with it, and the further that baton travels in time, the heavier the clichés become.

MISS AMERICA
- A BDSM
VAMPIRE TALE

Chrissie Bentley

Author Chrissie Bentley's 2012 novel *Miss America* clashes classical mythology
with modern eroticism for an outcome that is truly shocking.
(Courtesy of Chrissie Bentley)

4

LOVE BITES: ACCOUNTS OF THE VAMPIRE IN EROTICA

Charlaine Harris's Southern Vampire saga, the printed counterpart to the *True Blood* TV series, creates a universe in which sex—sometimes sensuous, sometimes searing, and sometimes so hot that it'll never make the small screen—is never far away from the action. Such eroticism is implicit in modern vampire stories in general, and Bram Stoker's *Dracula* in particular, but it was rarely even suggested in the earliest attempts to bring vampirism to the silver screen, although it was unquestionably—and deliberately—in place.

The revelation, in 1936, that there was a *Dracula's Daughter* was the cinema's first overt suggestion that sex played any part whatsoever in a vampire's customary lifestyle, and for a long time, it lived alone. Director Herbert L. Strock's 1957 *Blood of Dracula* movie may have been set in an all-girls' school, with all the connotations that surely spells, but such a location pandered more to its audience's libido than to its titular hero's.

It was with the arrival on the scene of the British Hammer studios, and a return to the girl's-school scenario for 1960's *Brides of Dracula*, that the old count was finally revealed for the sexual allegory that learned commentators now insist he always has been. By the late 1960s, in both film and book, physical desire was as much a part of the vampire legend as blood lust, and by the time Anne Rice's spellbinding novel *Interview with the Vampire* came along in 1976 to completely revitalize what had sadly become a very weary genre, the book's candid overtones of sexuality were probably the least surprising element in the entire tale.

Erotic author Chrissie Bentley explains, "The vampire story is the ultimate erotic adventure. It has everything: dominance and submission, willing surrender and willful possession; the thrill of the unknown and the thrill of being unknowing. It is the story of the innocent virgin facing her very first time, knowing that she will never be, or feel, the same again."

Bentley has told several erotic vampire stories. In "Death by V," one of the excellent short stores featured in the anthology *The Visitor* (HarperCollins/Mischief, 2012), a new breed of female vampire emerges, one whose fangs are placed somewhat lower down the body than they normally are, and whose chosen bitable body part is, likewise, positioned elsewhere. In "Taste the Blood of Dracula," a female descendant of the original count sets out to avenge herself on a film crew as it works on an especially tawdry remake of the 1970s movie of that same title. And in the full-length novel *Miss America*, the cult of our old friend Empousa is revealed to be alive and well in modern society.

Three very different takes on the legend, then, but three extremes that illustrate just how far the vampire itself has travelled in the century-plus since *Dracula*, not to mention how far erotica has come.

As I write this in the early spring of 2013, the publishing success story of the past year was indisputably the *Shades of Grey* trilogy, British author E. L. James's forty-million-plus-selling saga of BDSM-themed erotica—which, for readers with an eye for cultural verisimilitude, is set to do for erotic literature everything that *Deep Throat* did for erotic film. That is, allow everyone to think they can create it, flood the market with barely tolerable knock-offs and copycats, and finally, at the end of the day, trust that sufficient quality will rise to the surface to ensure that an entire generation won't be turned off sex forever.

Perhaps the most fascinating aspect of the entire story, however, is not the content of the books (which is, in all honesty, fairly humdrum when compared with much else that is out there), but its genesis. The *Fifty Shades* series started life as *Master of the Universe* and existed within the twilit world of *Twilight* fan fiction, continuing the adventures of the human Bella Swan and her vampire beau Edward Cullen beyond the realms of original creator Stephenie Meyer's own writings.

Far beyond. *Twilight*, for better or worse, exists in a universe that is devoid of sex—one where even the horniest vampire will merely flirt lightly with his victims, negating, in other words, what has been a critical aspect of literary vampirism for almost a century and a half. E. L. James, or Snowqueen's Icedragon as she termed herself in her original pseudonymous postings, snatched the libido back, examining in detail the sexual exploits of Edward and Bella. So much detail that some visitors to the fan-fiction websites upon which the stories were originally published began to grow a little squeamish. James removed the stories and republished them on her own website, before commencing a major rewrite that effectively expunged every last reference to *Twilight* from the tale. Edward and Bella became Christian Grey and Anastasia Steele, vampirism became sexual dominance and submission, and while the setting of the Pacific Northwest did not change, a whole new chapter of publishing history was about to be written.

At the same time, a far older one wondered what on Earth had hit it.

CARMILLA (1872)

Carmilla, Joseph Sheridan Le Fanu's classic tale of vampiric lesbianism, is Year Zero in the saga of vamp erotica. First published in the literary magazine *The Dark Blue*, it was (by the standards of the time) a daring work. Erotica, although it flourished throughout the late Victorian age, was very much the secret that nobody discussed, least of all those people who consumed and created it. It was published so far underground that you practically had to burrow to the center of the Earth to procure it. It was a world populated by seedy little men who populated seedy little shops, all tucked away in seedy little alleyways that no upstanding gentleman would even be seen whoring in. So they probably sent the butler instead.

Publishing, selling, mailing, even owning this kind of material was strictly illegal. So was writing it, and it is only over the last few decades that any of the myriad sexual writings from this era have received any kind of mainstream exposure, with many scholars viewing them less as erotic expositions than as studies in bedroom anthropology—an indication of just how greatly tastes have changed in the past century or so. Unless, of course, you happen to be into steampunk.

Le Fanu's writings are not explicit. His language could not in any way be compared to such classics as *Venus in India*, *My Secret Life*, or any other now-excavated treasure of nineteenth-century erotica. But *Carmilla* remains in their company regardless, as Le Fanu circumvented the myriad cultural and legal prohibitions that engulfed period erotica by ensuring that it existed only by inference, and even there was readily camouflaged. Nevertheless, the titular Carmilla's attraction only to other females, beginning with Laura (inhabitant of a magnificently Radcliffe-ian castle in the forests of southeastern Austria), leaves little to the prurient imagination—any more than the girl's persistent dreams of being bitten on the breast by a black, catlike creature whose fangs never leave a visible wound permit any doubt as to the nature of her visitor.

Carmilla is everything that a pre-*Dracula* vampire should be. She sleeps in a coffin, and can (as we have just seen) transform herself into an animal. She is abroad primarily at night, but shows no fear of the sun; she is staggeringly beautiful, and she has the ability to pass through solid walls. She is also very old, as Laura discovers when she happens upon a painting dated 1698. Although the subject's name is different, it is unmistakably a portrait of Carmilla.

Bram Stoker borrowed much from *Carmilla*, including the nature of her destruction—hunted down while she slept by a professional vampire hunter, Baron Vordenburg. Where he did not tread was into the most intimate corners of Le Fanu's haunt. Even at its most suggestive, *Dracula* remains fervently heterosexual. *Carmilla*, on the other hand, is avowedly lesbian.

Not quite shunned by the literati, *Carmilla* remained very much the lost sheep of Le Fanu's canon for many years, a short story dwarfed by the behemoths that were the novels *Uncle Silas*, *The House by the Churchyard*, and *The Rose and the Key*. However, it did make its way into the short-story collection *In a Glass Darkly*, alongside four other excellent mystery/horror tales, and from there, *Carmilla*'s influence slowly started to percolate.

In 1932, her tale was credited as a source for Carl Dreyer's masterpiece of expressionist exploration, *Vampyr*, the inspiration behind that movie's deployment of a woman as the vampiric focus. Thirty years later, Carmilla lent her name to the heroine of Roger Vadim's epic *Blood and Roses*. But it was not until 1970—that is, close to the centenary of her creation—that Carmilla truly took her place at the forefront of cultural vampirism, when the Hammer movie studio commenced the production of what would become a trilogy of lesbian vampire movies. *Vampire Lovers* (1970), *Lust for a Vampire* (1971), and *Twins of Evil* (1971) were all loosely (very loosely) based upon Carmilla's story.

At which point a second female fiend, this time drawn from history itself, was introduced to the cultural fray.

COUNTESS BATHORY

Hammer's *Countess Dracula* (1971) was rooted (also very tentatively, it must be admitted) in the story of Elisabeth, Countess Bathory, a sixteenth-century Hungarian noblewoman who was the source of considerable gossip around her hometown on account of the number of beautiful young women who seemed to enter her castle on a variety of pretexts and were never to be seen or heard from again.

Perhaps we hear a foreboding harbinger of Mary Elizabeth Braddon's *Good Lady Ducayne* here? Or not. Milady drained her victims, of course she did, but she did so for sustenance. According to the superstitious villagers who lived around Castle Bathory, Elisabeth required the blood merely to bathe in, as a means of maintaining her beauty and youth. What was even more shocking, however, was what she did with her victims *before* she killed them, torturing them to death in a variety of grisly and, it was whispered, sickly sexual ways.

Sometimes, she would often use her own teeth and jaws to rip the flesh of her victims. Other times, she would dress as a man and rape them with sundry detachable appendages. And for as long as she concentrated her depredations on peasants and commoners, nobody in authority paid Elisabeth's activities any attention whatsoever. But then the daughters of her fellow nobility began to disappear in a similar fashion, all popping over to Elisabeth's for one reason or another and never being heard of again.

The countess was finally arrested, at which point it became clear that all of the rumors about her and her ghastly appetites were true. Several of her accomplices were executed; the countess herself was condemned to life imprisonment inside her own castle, where she died in 1615. And according to some legends, she promptly started walking again.

The finest document of Elisabeth's peculiar tastes, at least for readers with an even stronger stomach than the average vampire novel requires, is Tony Thorne's *Countess Dracula: The Life and Times of Elisabeth Bathory, the Blood Countess* (Bloomsbury Publishing, 1997). Similarly chilling, if less historically detailed, is *The Bloody Countess*, a 1971 work by the Argentine poet Alejandra Pizarnik. And then there is "Daughter of the Night," a short story by Elaine Bergstrom, first published in 1992 and collected the following year in Pam Keesey's anthology *Daughters of Darkness: Lesbian Vampire Tales* (Cleis Books, 1993).

"Daughter of the Night" inverts the Bathory legend from both the sometimes-gratuitous horror of Thorne's account and the bored pathos of Pizarnik's to look at life through Elisabeth's eyes, in search of sympathy and perhaps even pity. And in so doing, it becomes even more disturbing than its predecessors. Because that's something that we often seek in erotic vampire stories but are not always granted: a sense of disturbance, of our own reality being swept imperiously aside in favor of another being's entirely.

Writer Jenny Swallows, a reviewer at EdenFantasys.com, very much captured the nature of modern vampire erotica, lesbian and otherwise, in her (otherwise glowing) review of another collection, *Girls Who Bite* (Cleis Books, 2011):

"Vampires. Has any supernatural being had such a bad time of things as the dear old vamp? If it's not the Anne Rice generation moping gloomily over the unbearable darkness of being, it's *la belle* Lugosi in the back row of film class, driving fresh stakes (or Stokers) into Nosferatu's heart. A new wave of *Twilight* tots playing emo bitey-neck while they watch *True Blood* reruns; and now, god help us, the Fifty Shades of fang fiction ghouls extracting the last shards of dentistry from a corpse that should have been buried ten years back."

Harsh words, but ones that do ring true in a universe where the vampire's bite is often regarded as a genre-pleasing substitute for traditional penetration, and the vamp's true talent for slow seduction and absolute absorption is reduced to little more than a form of foreplay. Whereas a good storyteller knows that it should be the other way around.

Daughters of Darkness dances in that direction with the inclusion of Robbi Sommers's "Lilith" and Jewelle Gomez's "Louisiana 1850," two stories that also remind us just how readily we have accepted the transition of the vampire from the old world of Transylvania-and-thereabouts to the new world of New Orleans and Louisiana—a feat that many may lay at the feet of Anne Rice, but which has its own historical verisimilitude too. A number of vampire superstitions traveled to the old Louisiana Territory aboard the ships that dumped France's convicts and hookers on the swampy, forested shores of Lake Pontchartrain, and tourists can still visit the Casa Do Diablo, from whence the city's earliest documented vampire would sally his vicious way down the Rue Bourbon in the 1830s.

But vampires can, and do, turn up everywhere, and a great vampire story knows it. Rhode Island and its border with Connecticut were rife with such legends in the eighteenth and early nineteenth centuries, and as late as 1892, a Rhode Island father, Mr. Brown, had his deceased nineteen-year-old daughter, Mercy, exhumed, so that her heart could be cut out and burned to halt her vampiric wanderings.

Further afield, elements of *Dracula* take place in Whitby, a beautiful but not necessarily haunting town on England's northwestern coast; and while the New England of Stephen King's imagination is automatically going to become a nexus of unforetold weirdness, still there was something almost homely about 'Salem's Lot before that mean old vampire set up shop there.

A short story by Anna Black, "The Temptation of Mlle. Marielle Doucette" (find it in D. L. King's *The Sweetest Kiss: Ravishing Vampire Erotica*—Cleis Press, 2009), is set in post-Revolutionary France, with a vampire who disguises his true nature by allowing the locals to accuse him of being a descendant of the Marquis de Sade. Paisley Smith's "Dark Angel" (*Girls Who Bite*) pitches up in Berlin just months after Hitler seized power. And Anne Tourney's staggeringly beautiful "The Resurrection Rose" (*Bitten: Dark Erotic Stories*—Chronicle Books, 2009) takes place in a garden center near San Francisco.

And every time, we find ourselves forgetting to ask (although we know we should): What exactly happened? Did the vampire mold him- or herself to the surroundings? Or did the surroundings mold themselves to the vampire? Because the point where they meet is seamless. Or as Charlaine Harris told the New Zealand magazine *Woman's Weekly*, "I think the popularity of the vampire myth comes down to, after so many years, vampires finally got sex right."

ANITA BERBER

This is especially so in the case of "Dark Angel." Berlin in 1934 was very much a city in political flux, torn between the near-hedonistic urges of the preceding Weimar era and the new puritanism of the incoming Nazis. It was also, of course, the artistic heart of Germany, a city that pushed boundaries and moralities as far as any modern society had ever permitted them to be taken. A vampire could not fail to be impressed by the city's fall into decadence, nor by the brutality with which a now-powerful minority was attempting to haul it back out of the figurative gutter.

We catch a glimpse of these contradictions in an episode of the British TV series *Hex*, truly one of the greatest (if sadly underappreciated) supernatural shows of the twenty-first century; only there, it is a Biblical demon, a Nephilim, who embraces the culture. We see it too in *Cabaret*, the movie made of Christopher

Isherwood's *I Am a Camera*; in this instance, it is an Englishman's repressed sexuality that needs to be revealed. Most of all, however, we see it in the life and works of Anita Berber, a German dancer and cabaret performer whose work is perhaps best summed up in the subtitle of her biography by Mel Gordon, *The Seven Addictions and Five Professions of Anita Berber: Weimar Berlin's Priestess of Depravity* (Feral House, 2006). (A former lover preferred a far baser term: *Fahrstuhlnummer.* Roughly translated, it means she was the kind of girl who would have sex with a stranger in an elevator.)

Even though the country had no direct vampiric traditions of its own, Germany was no stranger to the vampire; German cinema was the first to translate both *Dracula* (as *Nosferatu*, 1922) and *Carmilla* (*Vampyr*, 1932) to film, and a handful of titular red herrings notwithstanding, one of the first to suggest there was any kind of cinematic mileage to be had from the old bloodsucker. Look again at stills from *The Cabinet of Dr. Caligari* (1920), director Robert Weine's legendary expressionist horror film. Actor Conrad Veidt might be playing a mass-murdering somnambulist. But his appearance is so straight-out-of-Styria that the British rock band Bauhaus had no hesitation whatsoever in appropriating his image for the sleeve to their single "Bela Lugosi's Dead."

Vampirism is in the eye of the beholder, then, and Weimar Germany beheld more than most. Anita Berber saw to that.

Sex, horror, perversion. The very ingredients that critics of modern horror claim drip bloodily from the genre's success are the same as those that Berber's foes accused her of exemplifying ninety years ago. The difference is, Berber agreed with their condemnations, and regretted only that she could not go even further than she did. At least in public. Private performances, which she regularly staged, were rumored to have been tantamount to Bacchanalia.

She specialized in the grotesque, performed with a grace and beauty whose impact was only heightened by its lust for degradation. Shortly after marrying her openly gay husband Sebastian Droste in 1922, Berber presented a sequence of eleven new routines ("a unique evening," declared the advertisements) titled *Die Tänze des*

Lasters, des Grauens und der Ekstase—Dances of Vice, Horror and Ecstasy: "The Byzantine Whip Dance," "Cocaine," "Martyr," "Morphine," "Lunatic Asylum," "Suicide." Other routines in the years before Berber's death in 1928 included "The Corpse on the Dissecting Table," "The Somnambulist and the Convict," "Astarte," and "The Night of Borgia." The last-named of these concluded with her performing stark naked onstage, before an audience that included her character's father.

All of this has little (a certain resonance notwithstanding) to do with vampires directly. But her audience had no doubt as to Berber's true nature, this pansexual predator who lived by night; who subsisted on a diet of cognac and cocaine; whose naked body was on seemingly permanent exhibition; whose very sexuality, physical and emotional, was as much a part of her dance as her costumes and limbs, and was as contorted and deformed as the shapes into which she would twist herself.

Who danced death as readily as incest; whose personal life was her public persona. And who tore her lovers to shreds, figuratively if not literally. When the artist Otto Dix painted Berber's portrait, he saw her not as a woman in her mid-twenties at the height of her coke- and booze-addled beauty (for she was beautiful, all the surviving photographs and film attest to that fact), but as a broken crone of sixty or more. As a vampire.

TRU: A XXX PARODY (2010)

It has been said that a society gets the culture that it deserves, and that the lower the moral standards of that culture, the more debased that society ultimately is. Looking back at the life and especially the times of Anita Berber, learned historians might nod in weary agreement. Investigating the times in which we live today, one rather hopes that they might disagree—or at least, that the jury will stay out.

The adult movie industry has rarely, if ever, considered any topic off limits to its maker's fertile imaginings—from the 1920s stag reel *A Free Ride*, with its weather eye on the emergent mass popularity of the motorcar, to 2008's *Who's Naylin Paylin*, imagining an admittedly raucous day in the life of the then-headline-worthy Republican vice presidential nominee.

XXX parodies of current and classic TV shows and movies have been a staple of the industry for most of the twenty-first century, the nurturer of some of the highest-grossing (and biggest budget) porn movies of all time. A far cry indeed from the days when all that was required were a mattress, a lock-up, and a guy with a camera, but also a reminder that "If you build it, they will come." At a time when mainstream Hollywood was seriously feeling the bite of recession, its adult shadow was simply raking in the bucks.

Among these, one of the genuine highlights washed up in the veritable tsunami of parodies that leaped aboard the cash cow, *Tru* emerged a surprisingly adept stab at reading through the lines of the TV series (or at least season 1, which was as far as HBO had taken it at the time of conception), picking up from the cliffhanging discovery of a corpse in Detective Andy Bellefleur's car and making the same assumption that the rest of us did, that it was the mortal remains of Lafayette.

From there, *Tru* traces Sookie (Ashlynn Brooke)'s attempts to discover the identity of the murderer, racing through an only marginally parallel world in which brother Jason, bar owner Sam, and best friend Tara fight, flirt, and flap around as much as they ever did in the "real" show, and seemingly come together only to criticize Sookie's taste in men. Bill Compton is as suave and Southern gent–like as he ought to be; Eric Northman is as bad-temperedly foppish as he ought to be; and there is even a flashback appearance for Amy, the sadly murdered love of Jason's life, in one of the half dozen or so XXX scenes that are interspersed throughout the storytelling.

The characterization throughout the movie is excellent, individual mannerisms coming across not in the costume and wigs department (Eric's resembles a badly aligned crepe) but in little conversational asides. When Sookie, as perkily irritating here as she ever was on television, requests the day off to visit Bill, Sam unhesitatingly points out that that yes, it *is* day. So she probably won't see much of him. Pam packs as many lazy put-downs here as she does on

the small screen, Eric remains as laconically arrogant, and Tara...
yes, Tara's as obnoxiously argumentative as ever. Even Marianne,
whose true significance to the story had yet to be revealed at the
end of season 1, comes over as a mystifying delight, capable of
scaring the pants off Sam before she has even begun to vibrate.

In keeping with its intended audience, *Tru*'s sex scenes devour
far more of the movie's two-hour-plus running time than Sookie's
quest for justice. What is left, however, at least represents a regular
episode's worth of plot, with the ultimate reveal serving up a
surprise that is both genuinely unexpected *and* a wryly twisted take
on one of the climaxes that marked out the final chapter of the real
season 1. If you like *True Blood*, you may not love *Tru*. But if you
wish the cable show could be as steamy as the storyline sometimes
suggests it would like to be, then here's your dream come true.

British rock band Siouxsie and the Banshees always eschewed attempts to call them a goth band. But their first B-side, "Voices" (1978), is haunted by vampiric vapors. (Photofest)

5

BLOOD ON THE TRACKS: OR, AN IPOD FULL OF FANGS (PART 1)

"BAD THINGS"—JACE EVERETT (2006)

It was Anne Rice who popularized the possibility that a gang of timeless nosferatus were running loose round Louisiana, back in 1976 when she staked the Vampire Lestat into the heart of New Orleans. But it was not geographical convenience alone that prompted her to do so. The city and its surroundings not only knew the kiss of the vampire, they welcomed it. Because it made them feel at home.

That's the great thing about the opening credits to *True Blood*, that patchwork of old home movies, news clips, and photographs: the rotting shack, the waiting gator, the posing Klansmen, the roadkill possum. Sure, they nail down every Northerner's perception of the South. But they also pinpoint a lot of the things that every Southerner loves about the place. A way of life that doesn't care a hoot for the world beyond. Because the world beyond is not in the South. The world beyond could not have created "Bad Things." Or more accurately, it could not have shown us what "Bad Things" really were.

As is so often the case, the composer of what many people now think of as the archetypal Louisiana vamp song is not a native Louisianan, just as those creators of the ultimate bayou sound, Creedence Clearwater Revival, had never set foot in the bayou before they started singing about it. Indiana-born and raised, country singer Jace Everett recorded "Bad Things" during the sessions for his eponymous debut album in 2005. And that is where it might well have remained had the song not been selected as the iTunes Single of the Week one day in 2006. Cue an estimated 210,000 downloads, including one by Alan Ball, the creator of a new show that had just gone into production at HBO, *True Blood*.

Ball never intended to use the song in the show, and certainly never saw it as the program's opening theme. It just happened that way, when he grafted "Bad Things" onto the opening credits as a way of filling an empty space until something better came along. But nothing better *did* come along, so it stayed. Now it's hard to imagine anything else having even been considered.

Vampires were far from Everett's mind when he wrote the song. He was more interested in retrieving a bad loan from some guy he knew, and the song's original themes were violence and vengeance. In the original lyric, he wanted to do bad things *to* you. But he carried on playing, riffing around a twisted take on Steve Earle's "Poor Boy," listening as a switch to a minor key sent the vibe spiraling into darkness, and suddenly realizing that the song was sounding more sexy than scary. One minor word change later, the bad things he wanted to do *to* you became the equally bad things he would do *with* you. Big difference, meaningful difference.

"Bad Things" is a sexy, sleazy, spooky little song, and sewn into *True Blood*'s opening credits, it seethes and steams with such electrifying intent that you almost hope it will just shut up and get on with the bad things already. And the fact that it doesn't just piles enigma onto the aura of ill intent. Besides, "Bad Things" is by no means the only, or even the greatest, musical highlight in the annals of *True Blood*. As much as any other show in television history, *True Blood* revolves around its soundtrack, and does so with such beguiling style that most of the time you're not even aware of it. Until you're listening to the radio one day, and a song comes on that you only barely half recognize. And then the flashbacks begin.

The majority of the songs that follow have all played their part in soundtracking the series—if not directly, then at least by association. As for the handful that haven't, well, there's always next season. And the season after that....

"DEAD FLOWERS"—THE ROLLING STONES (1971)

Well, if you were borrowing a pagan demigoddess's Jaguar on your way to pick up a new shower pump, what would *you* expect the radio to play? Tara and Eggs were too bound up in themselves to notice, but the Stones' "Dead Flowers" is one of that band's most startling accomplishments, and a super crazy, creepy one at that.

Recorded during the nigh-on two years' worth of sessions that were eventually boiled down for the seminal *Sticky Fingers* album in 1971, "Dead Flowers" was an early manifestation of guitarist and cowriter Keith Richards's growing interest in country music. Not as an object of humor (see "Dear Doctor" on the earlier *Beggars Banquet* or "Faraway Eyes" on the subsequent *Some Girls*), but as a viable force to which the Stones were eminently capable of turning their hands.

It was not a popular move. *Rolling Stone*'s review of the album sniped, "The mere thought of the Stones doing straight country music is simply appalling. And they do it so poorly, especially the lead guitar." But the lyric itself is one of the Stones' darkest, not least for its sly references to heroin use, while singer Mick Jagger provides a fabulous counterpoint to the country twang by adopting his finest deep-fried southern blues vocal for the occasion. And what's more, it's a great song to sing along with.

"EVERYTHING IS BROKEN"—BOB DYLAN (1989)

Dylan is one of those rare artists who pops a couple of songs into the *True Blood* song track. "Beyond Here Lies Nothin'," which opens his 2009 album *Together Through Life*, is a neat R&B-themed stomper that danced through the trailers for season 2 and wound up the end credits once it was all over. But "Everything Is Broken" is the song that truly breathes in the ambience, haunting on so many different levels that even if Dylan had *not* admitted that it referenced his own relationship with the modern world, you'd know that something was amiss.

The song originally appeared on 1989's *Oh Mercy* album, a long-player that very much marked Dylan's resurrection following some extremely dodgy musical moves elsewhere in the 1980s. The single

"Political World" is generally regarded as the moment where we got our "old Dylan" back, but the battered-down vocal and the almost resentful guitar that traces "Everything Is Broken" to the grave can leave even the most disinterested listener feeling slightly uneasy.

Plus, the song has its own direct link with Louisiana. Dig out the 2008 collection *The Bootleg Series Vol. 8—Tell Tale Signs: Rare and Unreleased 1989–2006*, and thrill as an earlier and even more heartfelt rendition spirals out of a 1988 recording session in New Orleans. Everything was, indeed, broken. But this song, contrarily, fixed it all.

"REAL WILD CHILD"—JOAN JETT AND THE BLACKHEARTS (1997)

Jett's first band, the Runaways, are the runaway stars when Jessica and co. get their hands on the Guitar Hero game in season 5 (they run through Foreigner's "Feels Like the First Time" too, but let's not hold that against them). But Joan had already stamped her imprimatur on the show a season before, when her scathing rendition of an old 1950s rocker, which was in turn reinvented by Iggy Pop in the '80s, was chosen to accompany Tara's cage-fighting scene.

"Real Wild Child" is a brutal song, but it's a triumphant one as well, a declaration of teenaged piss and vinegar, rebellion and raucousness—the kind of rock song that makes you want to punch the air and shout your head off. Which, of course, is what happens every time Jett plays it in concert.

In an alternate scenario, another Jett classic, "Fetish," could ooze with equal resonance from the walls of Fangtasia, a vivaciously vivid rocker whose subject matter alone ensures it's unlikely to get played anyplace else, and that's before you confront its lurid lyricism. But we'll stick with "Real Wild Child" for now. It fits.

"FROM A WHISPER TO A SCREAM"—ALLEN TOUSSAINT (1970)

Allen Toussaint is the soul of Louisiana music. He is not the originator, nor its most active exponent. But when Toussaint speaks, the very bayou stops to listen, and when he records, time slows down.

Born in 1938, Toussaint wrote a stream of classic 1960s hits for Ernie K-Doe, Lee Dorsey, the Neville Brothers, Otis Redding, the Yardbirds, the Rolling Stones, the Hollies ... the list goes on. Then he launched a solo career in the early 1970s, and a clutch of excellent albums followed. "From a Whisper to a Scream" was the title track to the first, and when English singer Robert Palmer washed up in New Orleans four years later to record his debut solo album with Toussaint, "From a Whisper" was one of the first songs he wanted to tackle. "To me, that song was everything I wanted to find in New Orleans," Palmer said in the late 1980s, "and when I went further afield into the bayous, it was there as well"—in the sounds of the swamps, which truly can raise themselves from a sibilant hiss to an ear-piercing shriek; in the rush of the water as it follows storm and hurricane across all of man's conceits; and of course, in that last conversation you will ever have with a vamp, as it murmurs its intent with its mouth too close to your ear, and you reply with the last sound you will ever hear.

"VOICES"—SIOUXSIE AND THE BANSHEES (1978)

Wrapping up season 4, episode 8, Siouxsie and the Banshees' "Spellbound" was a natural theme for an episode that bore the same title. But it is not the band's sole contribution to our mythology. A hit in 1981, "Spellbound" was just one of the highlights of the group's fourth album, *JuJu*—the apex, says bassist and cofounder (with the eponymous Siouxsie) Steve Severin, of the band's flirtation with "gothic rock. There's more spooky imagery on *JuJu* [than on any of our other albums]."

"Spellbound" was astonishingly spooky. But track back three years, to a time when few people had any idea what to expect from Siouxsie and the Banshees, and we find them in a different headspace altogether. They were cutting their first single, and they knew they'd written a hit. So when it came to choosing a song for the B-side, Siouxsie and the Banshees decided to travel in the opposite direction entirely. "'Hong Kong Garden' with 'Voices' on the other side," Severin continues thoughtfully. "[That] is our ideal jukebox single. It could clear pubs."

It's true, too. It could. Guitars like a howling wind, percussion like a heart attack—"Voices" opens with adrenalin and urgency, and then, for no reason whatsoever, everything slows, everything halts, and suddenly Siouxsie's voice floats in from nowhere at all, hearing whispers from the window, hearing scratching from the inside, beckoning, calling, and echoing on the air.... Play it while reading that scene in *'Salem's Lot* when little Mark's dead friend Danny drops by to play. You will know exactly what she means.

Siouxsie and the Banshees' sound was difficult to define, even in its prime. The Banshees emerged out of punk rock, but their music echoed not rage and fury so much as vast gray concrete slabs of malnourished feedback, burning insects, screaming wires, and tortured twilight. It was the spaces in the songs that stunned, the wide-open gaps that hung haunting between every note, awaiting the banshee wail of Siouxsie's first vocal, or the last cry you might ever utter. *The Scream*, the band's debut album, did not simply isolate notes, it isolated every nuance of sound, from the mechanical *sturm und drang* of the almost frighteningly staccato "Metal Postcard" to the clinging, hanging howl that drapes across the rafters of the opening "Pure." And still nothing could prepare you for "Voices," six minutes of calculated malice, its effects-laden guitars and hypnotic staccato bespeaking a menace that was all the more palpable for Siouxsie's own deeply phased apparent uncertainty.

There was a distinct hint of Hitchcock (*Rebecca* comes to mind) in the atmosphere, and a trembling taste of Cathy and Heathcliff, freed by Kate Bush to haunt other quarters. But most of all, there was the sense that something new was happening; that someday, all music was going to sound like this. All worthwhile music, anyway.

"A lot of what we were doing," explains Severin, "if you have to put a name to it, was intended to be resonant, rather than innovative. We read a lot, we watched a lot of movies, and we tried to interest people in the same kind of things.

"A lot of it," he admits, "was just sort of accident, attempting to find something of our own. Our influences were the Roxy Musics, David Bowies, T. Rexes, a twisted sexuality, a black humor that was different. With the guitar we wouldn't say, 'Oh, you have to play an A-sharp minor there, and it'll be really spooky.' We'd say, 'Make it a cross between the Velvet Underground and the shower scene from *Psycho*.'"

"SEASON OF THE WITCH"—JULIE DRISCOLL, BRIAN AUGER & THE TRINITY (1968)

It was season 4 of *True Blood* that introduced this song to Bon Temps, in the hands of British-born actress, singer, and model Karen Elson. But it was already old long before that—and already magical too.

A remarkable beauty, Elson's career has taken her from the cover of the Italian *Vogue* on her eighteenth birthday, through a Nashville boutique and a host of TV ads, to a walk-on part at the 2012 London Olympics opening ceremony, membership of the New York cabaret troupe the Citizens Band, and a solo album, *The Ghost Who Walks*, produced by White Stripes' Jack White— her then-husband. She recorded a fascinating version of Serge Gainsbourg's "Je T'Aime" as a duet with Cat Power, was compared to Loretta Lynn by *Spin* magazine . . . and that brings us back to *True Blood* unveiling her version of "Season of the Witch," a song composed by Scottish folkie Donovan back in 1965, and that has since been subject to some of the most startling reinventions that any song could lay claim to.

Donovan's original version, it must be said, has little to do with its putative subject matter; he described it as his reaction to the kind of people he was meeting in his earliest years as a pop star, and the avarice and greed that propelled them. And the lyrics still tell that story. But somehow, the lyrics are immaterial today. It is the mood of the song, the slow building mystery of its accompaniment, the vast gulf of reinterpretation that the very melody lays bare to the enterprising performer (and listener) that intrigues, a process that began in 1968 when Julie Driscoll, Brian Auger & the Trinity recorded the song (for their debut album *Open*) and expanded it from the few short minutes that Donovan expended on it into over eight minutes of drama, expression, and fear.

Essentially a duet for vocal and Hammond organ, one riding a melody of its own beautification, the other pursuing and lapping the gymnastics around it, Driscoll's "Season of the Witch" is sexy and scary, moody and mellifluous, a Viking funeral in light jazz-rock costuming. It also completely reinvented the song.

Other artists grasped the nettle. Mike Bloomfield turned in a ferocious and even longer version before the decade was through; so did a British progressive band called Pesky Gee, shortly before they changed their name to Black Widow and scored a massive underground hit with "Come to the Sabbat." Richard Thompson, whose electrifying guitar was first heard on a 1967 Fairport Convention song called "It's Alright Ma, It's Only Witchcraft," covered "Season of the Witch" with a vocal frailty that was as resonant as his guitar was fiery; Dr. John, Courtney Love, Joan Jett, and Robert Plant have all made it their own as well. Movies have borrowed its title (often to ill effect, it must be mourned), and *Midnight Cowboy* author James Leo Herlihy took it for an excellent turn-of-the-sixties novel about a runaway girl named Gloria and transformed it into a virtual manifesto for the hippy generations to come.

Up against so many legends, Elson's version sounds a little sparse, a little self-conscious, a little too much like someone singing a song without quite grasping everything she's singing about. But maybe it's that which makes it work so well here. Sometimes a song can begin to creak if you think too much about all it entails. Elson's take may not be a patch on some of those that have gone before. But they enjoy its company, regardless.

"THE DREAMING DEAD"—JESSE SYKES AND THE SWEET HEREAFTER (2004)

The six-minute peak from Sykes and co.'s second album, *Oh My Girl*, in 2004 (following the priceless *Reckless Burning*), "The Dreaming Dead" is a guitar-heavy alt-country rocker, set aside from every other song that begs that appellation by Sykes's sweet vocal and the cool licks laid down by Phil Wandscher, with whom Sykes formed the band back in 2001.

With a sound that is as indebted to old psychedelia as it is to the modernistic bags into which the band are most frequently dropped, and with Sykes drawing a deeply romantic lyricism into view (one that shimmers not just on this track but on almost everything she touches), the group's strongest suit might well be the sheer majesty of their soundscapes. "I am not a musician or a song-writer in my innermost sanctum," Sykes tells visitors to her www.jessesykes.com website. "I'm more so a person trying to understand existence by attempting to create a visceral sonic experience with the elegance to depict the complexities of 'being'." "The Dreaming Dead" fits the bill with room to spare.

"RELEASE THE BATS"—THE BIRTHDAY PARTY (1981)

In London, 1980, the Birthday Party were never going to slip easily into any particular musical genre. Misfit Australian migrants, their visual assault of twisted Americana topped by fright wigs starched with static did at least nod toward prevalent street fashions.

But musically? Utterly cacophonous until (or unless) your ears finally made sense of the discordance and yelping, the Birthday Party polarized even the most forgiving audience. And they loathed the alacrity with which media and market alike slipped them into the then-fashionable gothic rock bag.

Attempts to praise them to their face were met with disdain, scorn, and rudeness; attempts to condemn them were greeted with ridicule. Calculated indeed was frontman Nick Cave's decision to write and record a cataclysm titled "Release the Bats."

It sounded like something Bela Lugosi would say. But only if he was sharing a cell with Renfield at the time.

"DON'T FEAR THE REAPER"—LYDIA LUNCH AND CLINT RUIN (1992)

Heaven 17 perform the song in *True Blood*, and the Blue Öyster Cult created it in the first place—guitarist Buck Dharma musing morbidly on the possibility of dying young, and pulling out a statistic that insists forty thousand men and women do the same thing every day. Shakespeare's Romeo and Juliet are his archetype, the ultimate star-crossed lovers in one of the greatest tragedies ever told. But "Don't Fear the Reaper" itself is not a tragedy. Rather, it is an inevitability, and one therefore that should not be feared—particularly if your fate happens to be that enjoyed by so many of the humans in and around *True Blood*.

So the Blue Öyster Cult's version is the most famous one, all chiming guitars and gentle vocals, cowbells, and axe solos—classic rock at its mid-1970s finest. But then Lunch came along in 1992, an Australian performance artist whose career only intersects with popular culture so that she can dismantle it, and an EP recorded with countryman Clint Ruin—a like-minded soul whose other identities include a stream of disturbing non sequiturs rooted around the unexpected use of the word *foetus*...You've Got Foetus on Your Breath, Foetus Under Glass, and most visceral of all, Scraping Foetus off the Wheel.

In their hands, everything that prompted *Rolling Stone* to name the original "Reaper" its Song of the Year for 1976 is put through the sonic wringer, to emerge a vast, bleak wall of sound, industrialized and intent on intensity, while Lunch's lead vocal almost lackadaisically dares the listener to try and adhere to the song's calming message. For there is nothing comforting or reassuring about this version. It is, however, dynamically sexy.

"ME AND THE DEVIL"—GIL SCOTT-HERON (2010)

There are *so many* great versions of this song—dating back to Robert Johnson's original blues lament in the early 1930s, and forward through the likes of Mick Jagger (on the soundtrack to *Performance*), Wild Willy Barrett, Peter Green, and Eric Clapton—that it seems almost sacrilegious to suggest that it took close to seventy years for a definitive version to appear. But Gil Scott-Heron, recording his final album before his death (2010's *I'm New Here*), pulled it off.

Four loping, groping, heart-pounding minutes of percussion, orchestration, and post-apoca-hip-hop drama carry the performance, scraping the mud of the old dirt track from the soles of Johnson's blighted shoes as it carries the song's message away from the country crossroads where the bluesmen met *his* devil (and traded his soul in exchange for stardom) and into the monochrome world of modern America, gray and gritty, fueled by poverty, fired by rage. The accompanying video, with its army of Mardi Gras dead men in the streets of the city, meanwhile, is probably the closest any pop video has ever come to the exquisite marriage of music and imagery that opens *True Blood*. But even with no more fanfare than one episode's closing credits, Scott-Heron takes his devil for a walk that neither is likely to forget.

"I WALK ON GILDED SPLINTERS"—DR. JOHN (1968)

The artist formerly known as Mac Rebennack was introduced to the world of *True Blood* with 1998's "I Don't Wanna Know," a latter-day Stonesy groove that "don't wanna know about evil," it "only wants to know about love." Which is nice to know. Nicer to know, though, is the music that Dr. John was making at the outset of his solo career, when he emerged from an apprenticeship playing sessions in New Orleans and Los Angeles at the helm of his own spellbinding creation: Dr. John the Night Tripper.

Dr. John was every local legend he had ever heard growing up in New Orleans, and every nocturnal terror with which his grandparents used to scare him to sleep. He grew up surrounded by the city's folklore; he was schooled in voodoo by its most legendary queens. With a background like that, he could have become a scholar, an academic, a tour guide…instead, he became a guitarist and then switched to piano after almost losing a finger in a fight. And slowly, he tired of playing on other folks' records and started dreaming of his own, a musical journey that would take everything he'd learned in Louisiana and all that he'd seen in Los Angeles and blend them into one cohesive whole—a whole that he called *Gris-Gris*.

Gris-Gris is the consummate American rock album of the late 1960s, primarily because it sounds like nothing that rock had ever done before. Voodoo rhythms snake and charm, vocals chant, and old charms are vocalized. The Doctor dressed the part too—

outrageous robes and towering feather dresses. His dancers writhed in the smoke of myriad potions; liquid lights bled fluid over the stage show. His very name, he explained, resurrected one of the legendary kings of New Orleans voodoo, and when *Gris-Gris* first fell upon an unsuspecting world, at least one reviewer claimed Dr. John was simply appropriating traditional voodoo chants and sacred music. He wasn't, but the intended insult was a compliment anyway. Because that is how real it all sounded.

You can dance through *Gris-Gris* and thrill at every turn. But it is the closing number that crystallizes the trip. "I Walk on Gilded Splinters" is the hand that grasps yours and draws you into the sacred heart of the religion and its rituals—to a place where you can smell the incense and hear the snakes, and Miss Jeanette's trailer in the backwoods of Bon Temps shakes to the earthquakes that the gilded splinters sent rattling forth, without a note of the music even playing in earshot.

Monstrous insects hiss and even bigger insects rattle. Something stirs in the undergrowth, and the overgrowth heaves in response. The darkness clings, the dampness pervades, the candles gutter, and the very ground lurches. A psilocybic gumbo nightmare, a Creole curse that bleeds even nonbelievers dry, "I Walk on Gilded Splinters" has earned a lot of covers over the years, and each one tells its own dark story. But Dr. John's is the granddaddy spider in the corner.

Step into its web.

"NUMBER ONE CRUSH"—GARBAGE (1995)

Some songs are too good for this world. "Number One Crush" is one of them. Garbage have already made their mark on *True Blood*, via the thumping joy of "Blood for Poppies." But had Jace Everett not got in there first, and the aforementioned *Hex* as well, "Number One Crush" would have made the ideal theme for the show and set the stage just as appealingly.

The song is creepy from the outset. In 1995, singer Shirley Manson told the UK magazine *Melody Maker*, "It's about somebody who wasn't *quite right*. Everybody's felt obsessive about something or somebody in their life. I've felt *crazy* about somebody before. That feeling—usually when you've split up with somebody—when you're absolutely obsessed with what they are doing." "I would die for you," swears the song's protagonist. But you get the feeling that [s]he might also require you to die as well. The song was, bandmate Butch Vig continued in that same interview, "disturbing."

But it was buried away on Garbage's first-ever B-side, and there it might have remained had it not been rescued for the soundtrack of the 1996 movie *Romeo + Juliet*. Remixed by Nelle Hooper, it became a radio hit in its own right. And eight years later, it soundtracked *Hex*.

Just two seasons were devoted to this astonishing show—two seasons in which the mood of the story shifted on an almost random basis, from a darkly amusing ghost story in episode 1, through a psychosexual drama a couple of episodes later that invoked the biblical Nephilim in the decidedly unbiblical surroundings of an upper-class English boarding school; on to the reanimation of a centuries-old legend of witchcraft; and—in time for the final conflict—the arrival of Ella Dee, the four-centuries-old daughter of Elizabethan-era alchemist John Dee, who has spent the intervening centuries hunting the Nephilim.

Erotically charged and psychologically scarred, *Hex* was not a critical hit, and it struggled in the ratings—so much so that it was cancelled at the end of the second season, with the story arc still awaiting resolution. Fans of the series poured scorn on the decision, but it also ensures that *Hex* lives on, undamaged by the ravages of longevity that have torn asunder other shows of similar ilk (*Buffy*, to name *Hex*'s most obvious comparison), nineteen hours of twenty-first-century British television at its very, very finest.

"SHE'S NOT THERE"—NEKO CASE AND NICK CAVE (2011)

Composed by band member Rod Argent, the original "She's Not There" was a monster hit for the Zombies in 1964, back in the days of the British Invasion. The group's name was not indicative of its nature—five handsome young men from St. Albans (the city, apropos of absolutely nothing, in which much of *Hex*, above, was filmed) were the sweetest sounding of all the bands of that era, and re-formed (we will not say *reanimated*), remain so today. Certainly nobody hearing "She's Not There," either at the time or on the oldies radio stations that have established it as one of the '60s' greatest hits, could ever have conceived of what Nick Cave and Neko Case might do to it close to fifty years later.

Cave we have already met: the voice of the Birthday Party, of "Release the Bats" fame above. Neko Case should require no introduction either; her years at the helm of the New Pornographers and a simultaneous career in the alt-country universe have established her as one of modern Americana's most distinctive voices.

Her union with Cave was conceived specifically for *True Blood*, a special event for the premiere of season 4 in 2011, and anybody who doubted whether Cave's uniquely sinister growl could ever dance comfortably with Case's soft cadence (a) obviously hadn't heard him singing with Kylie Minogue on his *Murder Ballads* album, and (b) didn't have a clue what the pair intended for "She's Not There."

It was a lament; now it is a threat. It was heartbreaking; now it is a heart attack. Case sings the song straight; Cave twists it around his fist and uses the chorus as a cudgel. Cynically, the reader could consider the whole thing a bit of a joke. But that would probably be before he or she has heard it. Of course "she's not there." She is running as fast as she can to get away.

"PARADISE CIRCUS"—MASSIVE ATTACK (2010)

Pioneers of the trip-hop musical form that took the dance scene by storm in the mid-1990s, Massive Attack were always worth more than any single genre could offer them—and part of the reason for that was the almost glacial pace at which they recorded new albums. No matter. The slow-burning "Paradise Circus" (as with the remainder of 2010's *Heligoland*) is quintessential Massive, with guest vocals by cowriter Hope Sandoval (of the American band Mazzy Star), and berths not only within season 3 of *True Blood* but also as the theme to the BBC's *Luther*.

"THAT SMELL"—LYNYRD SKYNYRD (1977)

"That Smell" was the highlight of what so tragically became the original Lynyrd Skynyrd's final album, 1977's *Street Survivors*. The record was still fresh on the shelves when the band's plane went down in a Mississippi swamp, and for those people who enjoy reading premonition into the lyrics of songs, "That Smell" immediately became a legend. "Tomorrow might not be here for you," sang vocalist and lyricist Ronnie Van Zant. "The smell of death surrounds you."

In fact, the song was written as a warning of the dangers of combining driving with either drink or drugs, after guitarist Gary Rossington was fortunate enough to survive a car crash under just those influences. Which itself was the latest in a series of increasingly reckless inci/accidents to have befallen the band as fame and fortune tore them from the bars of Jacksonville, Florida, to the stadia of the world.

Responsible for so many of classic rock's most sanctified anthems, from the eternal slow dance of "Free Bird" to the fist-pumping defiance of "Sweet Home Alabama," Skynyrd were (and remain; they re-formed around Rossington in 1987) one of the South's most enduring and exciting treasures. Certainly the jukebox at Merlotte's would be a lot less exciting without them.

"WHO DO YOU LOVE"—JUICY LUCY (1970)

Skynyrd's plane went down just outside McComb, Mississippi, a town that has just one other serious claim to rock 'n' roll legend. It was there, in 1928, that Bo Diddley was born. And Bo Diddley penned what is honestly, truly, and seriously the greatest song ever written about all the weird and wicked things that dwell in the swamps of the deepest South.

"Who Do You Love" was Diddley's retort to Muddy Waters' recent "I'm Your Hoochie Coochie Man," with the protagonist's strength and darkness bound up in his "black cat bone." Bo wanted more, a super-badness that would not only impress the chicks, it would frighten off their boyfriends too. Would *you* want to mess with a guy who used cobras for a necktie and went around kissing boa constrictors? Allying the imagery with a chant that he heard some kids singing on the streets of Kansas City, he set out to create the meanest, roughest slice of R&B that anyone had ever heard.

He succeeded. The protagonist of "Who Do You Love" walks miles of barbed wire. His necktie is a cobra snake; he lives in a house made from human skulls. He reeks of death and it clings to his coat-tails, so even after he has passed, to paraphrase Shakespeare, you know that something wicked this way passed.

"Who Do You Love," like "I Walk on Gilded Splinters" and "Season of the Witch," is one of those songs that gains a little something with every retelling. The Doors used to play it when Jim Morrison was at the height of his leather-dripping Mr. Mojo Rising phase, and the lyrics spun from his lips like autobiography. The Quicksilver Messenger Service took it and transformed it into the sidelong freak-out that defined their debut album. But it was an Anglo-American band, Juicy Lucy, that truly nailed the song.

Formed by slide guitarist Glenn Ross Campbell, relocated to the UK from his native California, and black Londoner Ray Owen, Juicy Lucy were cutting their debut album in 1970 when Owen was hit by a stinking cold. He went to the studio regardless, and the demands of the day ensured that he would have to perform. So he gravel-growled his way through Bo's most foreboding lyric and transformed it into something that sounded even more evil than that. Campbell's guitar got in on the game, twisting angrily, serpentine, around a rhythm that rattled like the ice truck that whips around the song's parched-dirt tracks, and "Who Do You Love" was utterly reborn.

Do *not* play it loud with the lights out.

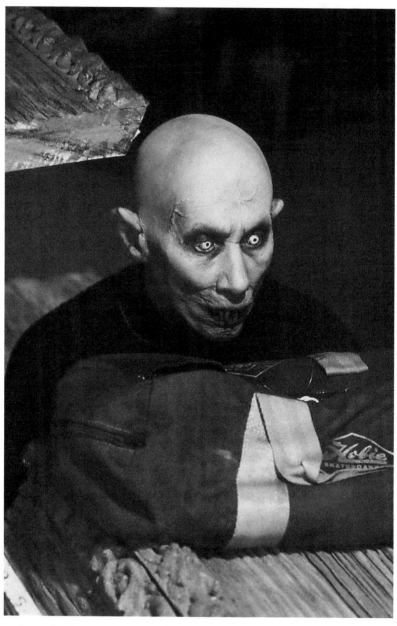

An ancient horror comes to modern New England. Stephen King's *'Salem's Lot*
hit primetime TV in 1979. (CBS/Photofest)

6

MANUSCRIPTS DON'T BURN: FURTHER FICTION, FRICTION, AND FANGS

THE ADVENTURE OF THE SUSSEX VAMPIRE —ARTHUR CONAN DOYLE (1924)

Among the multitude of contemporary critics who raised their voices to praise the original publication of Bram Stoker's *Dracula*, few were as vociferous as Arthur Conan Doyle. It helped, or maybe it didn't even matter, that he was already a friend of Stoker's. A man who was not much given to widely praising anything nevertheless saw in *Dracula* the same qualities that he valued in his own writings, and not necessarily in those stories for which he is best remembered today.

Celebrating his seventy-first birthday (in 1930) with an admirable fit of pique, Conan Doyle allegedly snapped how sick he was at hearing himself described as the author of the *Sherlock Holmes* stories. "Why not, for a change, the author of *Rodney Stone* or *The White Company* or *The Lost World*? One would think I had written nothing but detective stories."

In fact, Conan Doyle had spent his career writing about just about anything that took his fancy, and a vast corpus of occult tales can be numbered among that company. A lot of nonsense as well, as he devoted the last fifteen or so years of his life to singing the praises of spiritualism, spirit photography, fairies in the garden, and almost any other fanciful notions that twentieth-century tomfoolery could fling at him.

His interest in the supernatural, however, could be traced through many more of his writings than those last few years of credulity. Back in 1892, before either he or Stoker had achieved any kind of literary fame, the pair contributed chapters to a magnificent literary conceit called *The Fate of Fenella*, in which no fewer than twenty-four little-known novelists conjured a novel of deliciously preposterous gothic pretensions. *The Lost World*, published in 1912, was successful enough to make its first appearance on the silver screen in 1925, and of course Sherlock Holmes had his own brushes with the inexplicable, not least of which was the quasi-werewolf that is the hound of the Baskervilles.

The old master's most redolent tale, however, must be *The Adventure of the Sussex Vampire*—one of the twelve included in 1924's *The Case Book of Sherlock Holmes*, and a story that has been cited by more than one learned Holmesian scholar as Conan Doyle's personal tribute to (or perhaps, parody of) *Dracula*.

It features all the necessary ingredients for a good vampire tale: A child, mysteriously weakening and bearing the twin telltale fang marks on his throat. His mysterious South American mother, who is seen by the nurse with her mouth sucking at the boy's throat. And Holmes, the master of logic and common sense, apparently battling with the realization that here, for once, is a case that defies all of his learning and erudition. But what, he asks his faithful sidekick Doctor Watson at the outset of the tale, "What have we to do with walking corpses who can only be held in their graves by stakes driven through their hearts? It's pure lunacy."

And so it proved, as the vampire turned out to be a fifteen-year-old boy, jealous of the half brother his newly remarried father has just foisted upon him, and amusing himself by firing poison darts into the infant's neck. Poisoned his stepmother then dutifully sucked out of the wounds, to prevent her husband from discovering just what a nasty little brat he had sired during his first marriage.

Such a down-to-earth (if, simultaneously, utterly fanciful) solution to what could have been a very jolly romp through the undead denizens of the English countryside has not, of course, stilled the voices of those who will seek out arcane meaning from every word Conan Doyle wrote. Wryly, one might note, there has even been a volume published that is devoted wholly to Conan Doyle's "vampire stories" without one of the tales therein actually involving anything remotely resembling a vampire. And other writings not only discuss Holmes's relationship with the characters in Stoker's novel but even suggest that the detective and the vampire had come to a certain arrangement, under whose terms neither would do anything that impinged upon the other's territory. Loren D. Estleman's 1978 novel *Sherlock Holmes Versus Dracula, or The Adventure of the Sanguinary Count* is a profoundly authentic-feeling romp through one such encounter that notes, very imaginatively, that Holmes and Dracula took their respective bows onto the streets of London more or less simultaneously, and that one could not have helped but notice the existence of the other.

Holmes, incidentally, is no less dismissive of the supernatural here than he is in Conan Doyle's original writings.

THE MASTER AND MARGARITA—MIKHAIL BULGAKOV (1940)

Mikhail Bulgakov's *The Master and Margarita* is not a vampire story. It does, however, feature one of modern literature's most alluring vampires. Hella arrives in late-1930s Moscow as one of the terrifying retinue of lieutenants accompanying the Devil on what initially seems to be nothing more than a mischief-making jaunt. Booking himself into a theater as the magician Woland, the Prince of Darkness then makes his rampaging way through some of the city's leading intellectual hypocrites, while simultaneously pulling strings on the apparently doomed romance between the titular characters: a beautiful woman named Margarita and her lover, a suppressed novelist whom she has named the Master.

Named for a Russian tradition that applies the term to girls who die young and are transformed into vampires as a consequence, Hella does not have the greatest role to play in the drama that unfolds, upstaged by a wall-eyed demon named Azazello and a giant, walking, talking black cat called Behemoth. But when she does appear, she is unforgettable.

She is generally sighted completely naked, although on one occasion she prefers a lacy apron, white cap, and golden slippers.

Blessed with a perfect figure, she is "a redhead with eyes that burned with a phosphorescent glitter" and possesses a touch that is "cold as ice." Her eyes are green, and so are her fingers, "green and cadaverous." There are patches of decay on her breast, and there is a livid scar on her neck. Rarely, however, does one victim take all this in at once. She never allows them the time to study her.

> *"Let me give you a kiss," said the girl tenderly, her gleaming eyes close to his. Varenukha lost consciousness before he could feel her kiss.*

And when next we see Varenukha, he casts no shadow, and he and Hella are delighting themselves by terrorizing somebody else. Later in the story, Hella supervises Margarita's preparations prior to the Devil's midnight ball, bathing the bemused woman in blood.

Those are Hella's sole roles in the story, although we know from author Bulgakov's notes and the memories of his wife Elena that the story was never completed to his satisfaction, and that more might well have been planned for this most uncanny of nocturnal visitants. Yet there is also a mysterious nonending to her tale. When Woland and his minions finally depart Moscow, Hella is not among them. Perhaps she stalks the city still?

I AM LEGEND—RICHARD MATHESON (1954)

It has been described as the first vampire novel of the modern (that is, post–World War II) era, yet its best-known influence was on George A. Romero's *Night of the Living Dead*. It is an epic of survivalism set in a postapocalyptic world, yet it has been described as the first novel since *Robinson Crusoe* to truly get to the heart of human loneliness. And it has been made into so many movies in its own right (four: Vincent Price's *The Last Man on Earth* [1964], Charlton Heston's *The Omega Man* [1971], Will Smith's *I Am Legend* [2007], and the same year's *I Am Omega*) that it is easy to forget that the protagonists of the original story are even vampires to begin with.

Assuming that that is what they are. Because *I Am Legend* is all of these things and more, and Matheson's vampires are as far from any gothic antecedent as they could be. Rather, he conjures creatures that are the victims of a global bacteriological pandemic, spread through the blood, and manifest, following a sufferer's death, in the reanimation of the corpse in search of fresh blood. Other effects, including an aversion to sunlight, adhere to vampiric stereotypes but are, again, simply a manifestation of the infection.

Robert Neville, the movie's human protagonist, *is* the last surviving uninfected human and is, therefore, prone to some startling bouts of Crusoe-esque loneliness. But his discovery of what he initially believes to be his own Girl Friday, Ruth, is crushed when he discovers that some of the infected are slowly beginning to overcome the plague's most dehumanizing aspects and are now building a new society in their own image—a society in which he is seen as being as alien to its people as "vampires" were to him. The book's title is taken from the last words Neville speaks before he is executed by his captors: "[I am] a new superstition entering the unassailable fortress of forever. I am legend."

In many ways, then, *I Am Legend* is no more a tale of vampiric doings than any of the myriad other stories of the final handful of human beings struggling to survive in a world that has been emptied of humanity, whatever the cause. The Martians of H. G. Wells's *War of the Worlds*, the titular plant life of John Wyndham's *The Day of the Triffids*, and the zombies that people everything from *Night of the Living Dead* to *The Walking Dead*—this is the family tree in which *I Am Legend* is most comfortable. Even the notion that vampirism could be spread by a disease is not unique to Matheson, with medical science musing over the possibility that certain historical manifestations of the condition might have a grounding in both the blood disorder porphyria (a theory that has now been debunked, but still circulates on the Internet) and rabies.

Matheson's new society can also be seen as a political allegory, to which vampire legend has long been allied—what is Dracula anyway, with his fine castle and servile servants, but any great lord of the manor, feeding on the lifeblood of the peasantry? Karl Marx, whose corpse numbers the Highgate Cemetery Vampire among its neighbors, routinely described capitalism as vampiric: "dead labor which ... lives only by sucking living labor, and lives the more, the more labor it sucks"; and a century before that, Voltaire noted how society was now ruled by "stock-jobbers, brokers, and men of business, who suck...the blood of the people in broad daylight."

The notion that only via an absolute apocalypse could a new world be birthed, again, is not unique to *I Am Legend*. (To name but one, *Planet of the Apes* employs a similar premise.) But almost two decades before the hippy movement arose with its own demand for the modern world to be torn apart and replaced by a return to some Utopian garden, *I Am Legend* reminded us to be careful what we wished for.

DRACULA—THE COMIC BOOK

The horror boom that grasped the American comic book by the throat in the early 1950s was a response to any number of external factors, not least of all the polarization of society around the distinct theme of goodies (us) and baddies (those no-good stinking Commie Reds) that hallmarked the Cold War.

That horror tended to reverse the order of things and allow the baddies to triumph over an awful lot of goodies before finally being put paid to in their own right was, perhaps, an early lesson in the ways of the real world for many young readers. But it made for thrilling reading, and in the world of comic horror, Atlas Comics led the way. EC Comics would later surpass them, of course, to become the definitive purveyor of American horror comics. But months before *The Haunt of Terror* and *Tales from the Crypt* hit the stands, in December 1949, *Suspense* comic debuted, and its developing take on what a storyteller could and couldn't get away with in those days was one of the first steps down the rocky road that would ultimately see the American comic industry become as emasculated by the comics code as Hollywood, two decades earlier, had been castrated by the motion-picture equivalent.

Suspense was seven issues old when Dracula made his first appearance, and for sure, he ignited a new taste in horror. But then

EC's Bill Gaines and Al Feldstein came along, and nothing could be the same again. Even their speech balloons could upset your stomach, as original readers of the 1953 strip "Midnight Mess" (from *Tales of the Crypt* #35) might recall.

A new restaurant has opened in town, and a young man named Harold has heard rumors that its staff and clientele alike are vampires—rumors that are swiftly proven correct.

"This restaurant serves blood dishes," he is informed. "Like a vegetarian restaurant serves vegetable dishes. Blood juice cocktail ... hot blood consommé ... roast blood clots ... French fried scabs ... blood sherbet." And the next thing Harold knows, he is suspended upside down from the ceiling, a tap has been inserted into his jugular, "and each of the vampires came one by one and filled its glass."

This was actually one of the more refined deaths dreamed up by the EC scribes. In "Strop! You're Killing Me," a fireman is slashed to ribbons when somebody replaces the descent pole with a razor blade. In "Hot Seat," Santa is burned to a crisp when he slides down a chimney into a waiting open fire. Etcetera, etcetera.

It was to put a stop to EC's antics that the comics code was developed in the first place. It kicked into action on October 26, 1954, and for the next close to twenty years, the nation's publishers obeyed its dictates religiously. Their wares could not be distributed to the comics trade if they did anything else (of the major publishers, only Dell Comics did not subscribe to the code, and celebrated by running a lightweight Dracula superhero comic during 1966–1967).

Naturally, there was constant pressure being placed on the code's enforcers to lighten the strictures they placed upon what could and couldn't be included in a comic book, but it was all in vain. It would be January 1971 before a concession was made, and many complained that it was but a fraction of what the industry had been demanding.

Still, it was one that lot of writers had been waiting for. Among the manifold prohibitions unleashed by the comics code had been a blanket ban on almost every classic horror creation you could name. Now the code's longstanding aversion was revised to permit the appearance of "vampires, ghouls, and werewolves" but only "when handled in the classic tradition."

Marvel Comics, the industry leaders that had developed out of the old Atlas imprint, promptly responded with the introduction of Michael Morbius, a scientist transformed into a living vampire while researching a cure for the rare blood disease with which he was afflicted. Maybe he was a far cry from the Dracula that his publishers had played with in the '40s. But he remained recognizably a colorfully garbed, red-eyed, and fanged vamp. Morbius initially popped up to terrorize readers of *The Amazing Spider-Man* that October, before settling down to his own long life in the Marvel Universe, one of that select handful of characters who can adeptly swing from good guy to bad depending upon the demands of the plot.

There would be no such equivocation for Marvel's next vampire, however. In 1972, the writer and artist team of Gerry Conway and Gene Colan sold editor Stan Lee on the idea of revisiting Dracula, not for a one-off appearance, however, but as the star of his own monthly comic book.

Lee agreed, and six months after Morbius was born, *The Tomb of Dracula, Lord of Vampires* made its debut with the first installment of what would ultimately run to seventy monthly issues (the title finally folded in August 1979). And it was apparent from the outset that life for the comic-book Drac was not going to differ too much from life for any of his predecessors. He is still pursued by a Van Helsing and a Harker, descendants (granddaughter Rachel and son Quincy respectively) of the original vampire hunters, and when Marvel launched companion titles *Werewolf by Night* and *Frankenstein's Monster*, Drac was an inevitable guest star.

The saga opens with "Night of the Vampire!," a dark and stormy night alive with "a stench of death, of things long past living," and a sound that drifts beneath the teeming rain, "the sound of a faltering engine ... the sound of a nightmare's birth!"

Frank Drake is the last living descendant of an ancient family line, visiting Transylvania to arrange the sale of the last surviving relic of the family's past wealth, a castle whose name was *not*

Americanized when the clan emigrated to the United States. Castle Dracula still stands, fearful and foreboding and empty, bar the battalion of bats that have seemingly taken up residence in every room.

A floor gives way, a tomb is discovered, a staked skeleton lies within. And when the stake is removed for a keepsake … "Dracula lives again!" Nor would the eventual cancellation of his comic prove any greater an obstacle to Dracula's continued life within the Marvel Universe than any of the deaths dealt out in movie or novel. He has reappeared in adventures featuring such vintage stalwarts as the Uncanny X-Men and Doctor Strange, while the 1990s brought the miniseries *Tomb of Dracula* and *Curse of Dracula*. And yes, Blade, who started life as very much a minor supporting character in the original *Tomb of Dracula* series, is the same chap who starred in three eponymous movies in the 2000s.

'SALEM'S LOT—STEPHEN KING (1975)

'Salem's Lot is Stephen King's masterpiece. It is not alone in that definition; any one of perhaps half a dozen of his novels could grasp a similar appellation, from the schoolgirl disturbances of *Carrie* (1974) to the haunted hotel–lit *The Shining* (1977), and on to such specialized terrors as *Cujo* the dog (1981), *Christine* the car (1983), and of course the leviathan *The Stand* (1978).

But somehow, *'Salem's Lot* bestrides them all.

King himself has cited *'Salem's Lot* as his favorite of all his novels, "because of what it says about small towns" (in an interview with Phil Konstantin in *The Highway Patrolman 1987*). But also because it proved, at a very early stage in his career, that he was as comfortable working within the traditional corners of the horror genre as he was reaching toward what would ultimately become ever more fantastical notions. That he proved himself eminently capable of then pulling those fantasticalities into the mainstream (honestly, was anybody *really* scared of clowns before they read *It*?) is immaterial here. Quite simply, *'Salem's Lot* returned the vampire story to the realms of serious literature after too many years—nay, decades—of languishing within the world of the pulps.

It was King's second novel, published in 1975 on the heels of *Carrie*'s runaway success, and in many ways it is both his most conventional and his farthest reaching. Briefly, it tells the story of a writer, Ben Mears, returning to the small New England town where he grew up and setting to work on a book about the town's lone landmark, a sprawling hilltop mansion known as the Marston House.

Mears is not the only new arrival in the town. Moving in around the same time is a pair of businessmen, an Austrian antiques dealer named Kurt Barlow, and his partner and front man, Richard Straker. Barlow, Straker patiently explains to all who inquire, is a recluse who is rarely seen at night.

And never seen during the day, it transpires.

Mears makes an unlikely Van Helsing, but it is to him that the role falls as a small cadre of townspeople (Mears's girlfriend, Susan; schoolteacher Matt Burke; the priest, Father Callahan; doctor Jimmy Cody; and an adolescent boy named Mark) realize that more or less the rest of their friends have either disappeared or taken to paying sinister nocturnal visits on their relatives.

While Susan is an early casualty in Mears's war against the bloodsuckers, and Callahan, Cody, and Burke are all picked off too, the writer and the teenager battle on and finally succeed in destroying Barlow. Which is where things become especially interesting. Vampire convention over the past century or so has insisted that when the master vamp is destroyed, so his creations, too, must perish. Why, nobody has ever really explained. But it does allow a plague of bloodsuckers to be cleared up in one fell swoop. In *'Salem's Lot*, they do not die, which does beg the question of what happens when all available food stocks have been depleted and a town is exclusively populated by vampires. What do they eat then?

That conundrum never has to be resolved. Not immediately anyway. Mears and Petrie flee, only to return a year later and burn the place to the ground. Presumably there were no survivors.

Although the once-threatened sequel to *'Salem's Lot* never materialized, King has continued to tinker with the concept. A pair of short stories, "Jerusalem's Lot" and "One for the Road," both offered further background to the town itself, while a 2005 illustrated edition (Centipede Press) allowed King to restore over fifty pages of material deleted from, or never truly visualized in the then thirty-year-old original edition. Gorier deaths, more violent vampires, longer conversations…nothing that detracts from the purity of the original book, but much that adds to the thrills, and much, too, that illustrates King's own description of the story as "*Peyton Place* meets *Dracula*."

The point that any discussion of *'Salem's Lot* will keep returning to, however, is its impact upon the horror genre in general and vampire fiction in particular. Both, by the mid-1970s, had more or less been consigned to the back burner of popular fiction, cheaply produced mass-market paperbacks of the type sold on dusty metal racks in the drug stores—poorly written (usually), badly edited (often), and gaudily packaged (always), and pumped out to meet an audience that mainstream publishing apparently regarded as beneath contempt. Killer crabs, cannibal crayfish, death-dealing dandelions—it was as though the '50s B-movie never went away.

Carrie nudged the genre back toward a degree of respectability, but it was *'Salem's Lot* that truly recreated horror as a major market force, largely because it restored reality and, for the duration of the story, real people to the genre. No more cyphers meeting their maker in increasingly imaginative manners; King's characters lived and breathed (the *Peyton Place* analogy is especially apt here), and in doing so, brought the Lot itself to life.

Even more astonishing was the sheer weight of characters whom we did come to know. In both *Carrie* and *The Shining*, the novels on either side of *'Salem's Lot*, King allowed his pen to focus on just a handful of protagonists, with the latter famously cutting a single family off from the rest of the world and allowing isolation, fear, and a slow, creeping madness to do the rest. *'Salem's Lot*, contrarily, was populated with a small town's worth of characters, and as fascinating as the vampiric aspects of the story are, equally compulsive is the effect that an unknown terror has on the masses, as opposed to the individual.

It was only later that King revealed that behind the fictional story of a ruthless vampire slaughtering everyday folk, there lay a real-life counterpart. His story was inspired by revelations breaking in the press about the then-incumbent President Nixon's own vampiric disregard for the niceties of decency, law, and the Constitution; the subterfuge and secrecy with which a paranoid White House was striking out at people it even suspected of being opposed to it; and the fear that it might (and indeed, would) take more than the scapegoating impeachment of a crooked president to bring the edifice to heel.

Arguably, Watergate was the worst thing to happen to American politics at that time, in that it permitted everybody involved in criminal government to shift the blame onto Nixon and then just carry on as before, undetected, knowing that "justice" had got its pound of flesh. *That* is why, when Barlow dies, the rest of the vampire clan lives on. Because sometimes, cutting off the monster's head is not enough. As Richard Matheson demonstrated a quarter century before, the rest of the system needs to be razed as well.

Deep thoughts. Certainly deeper than the average reader would expect him- or herself to be entertaining after reading a simple vampire story—and deeper than many wanted to go. King's career as a potential political analyst would never take off. His status as the emperor of American horror, however, was assured, and when November 1979 brought Warner Brothers TV's three-hour made-for-TV adaptation of *'Salem's Lot*, both the Edgar and the Primetime Emmys hastened to acknowledge it.

More recently (2009), *Entertainment Weekly* ranked actor Reggie Nalder's portrayal of Barlow as the eighth-greatest vampire of all time (Rutger Hauer played the same role in a 2004 remake), and even viewers who had cringed through David Soul (as Ben Mears)'s past careers as TV cop Hutch (in *Starsky and . . .*) and a chart-topping balladeer acknowledged that this time, he got it right.

Yet for all it achieved, and all of the praise, *'Salem's Lot* would remain the pinnacle of late twentieth-century vampire fiction for less than twelve months. For as deep in the South as the Lot is in the North, another mighty vampire was stirring. And he was giving interviews.

TEN GREAT VAMPIRE HOLIDAY DESTINATIONS

Dracula's Castle, Whitby, England

It was in the shadow of the East Cliff, and the East Pier that stretched dark and decaying out from beneath it, that the Russian schooner *Demeter* finally came to rest in Bram Stoker's *Dracula*. And what a sight she was, with her dead captain lashed to the wheel and her hold opening to reveal just one survivor, an immense dog that leaped from bow to sand and vanished into the old town. A legend had arrived on British shores, and the local tourist trade has not looked back.

The stately ruins of Whitby Abbey have been renamed in honor of the town's most famous fictional resident—a disservice, perhaps, to the stately pile's original purpose, but a boon to the tourist industry. The local church is firmly nailed to the Stoker legend, and when storms in early 2013 caused the adjacent cliffs to crumble and lay bare the inhabitants of the burial ground, you can guess what the headlines screamed. Gift stores and tea houses cater to the vampire hunter in us all, and when the storms blow in from the North Sea and the waves are whipped to a frenzy by the elements, you can sit in the comfort of your sea-view hotel room and maybe get a sense of what Bram Stoker felt when he wrote the story in the first place.

The Sofitel Hotel, West Hollywood

Visit Dallas, Texas, and you will search in vain for the Hotel Carmilla. But fly into Los Angeles and cab it to 8555 Beverly Boulevard, and you too can join the long line of visitors who have asked whether the hotel bar serves Tru Blood.

Bran Castle, Transylvania

An entire industry has grown up around Dracula in the Romanian province, with tour operators offering full weeks' worth of travels around the ancient land's most evocative landmarks. None of these have anything to do with Bram Stoker's original book, beyond maybe looking the part, but it is impossible not to be impressed by their majesty and scale regardless.

Plus, the tour guides tell such wonderful stories that it is impossible not to get carried away when standing in the lee of Bran Castle, on the road between Sighisoara (birthplace of Vlad the Impaler) and Poiana Brasov. The histories tell us it dates back to 1377, and it once hosted the heart of Queen Maria of Romania. Your imagination can fill in the rest.

Forks, Washington
You can drive by the high school that *Twilight* immortalized, but be aware that Forks itself has very little else of interest....

Cachtice Castle, Slovakia
Home to the Blood Countess, Elisabeth Bathory. You cannot quite walk the floors that were once bathed in blood, as the castle lies in ruins. But they can tell their own story just as well.

New Orleans, Louisiana
Until she moved away from the city in 2004, Anne Rice's house was high up on many tourists' agenda. So was the vacant lot wherein Lestat was finally imprisoned within his own reflection—and which is now a restaurant. But wander the streets and alleyways of the French Quarter anyway. You will not be disappointed.

Bram Stoker's House, Dublin, Ireland
The spirit of Bram Stoker still resides at 15 Marino Crescent, the house where he was born. Allegedly.

Lazzaretto Nuoco, Venice
The dead of Venice were buried not in the city itself but on the out-lying islands, and in 2010, an archaeological dig among the mass graves that testify to medieval outbreaks of the plague unearthed one corpse whose mouth had been crammed open with a brick. A sure sign, say the folklorists, that the locals believed her to have been a vampire.

Sadovaya Street, Moscow

We don't know the precise building. But somewhere on Sadovaya Street is the apartment building in which poor Rimsky, the theater treasurer, was terrorized to within an inch of his life by the vampires Hella and Varenukha in Bulgakov's *The Master and Margarita*.

Bray Studios, Maidenhead, England

Down Place, perched picturesquely on the banks of the River Thames, is the same majestic complex where many of the early (pre-1966) Hammer movies were shot.

INTERVIEW WITH THE VAMPIRE—ANNE RICE (1976)

Interview with the Vampire could not have been further opposed to *'Salem's Lot* if author Anne Rice had sat down with the King book and purposefully schemed its absolute corollary.

Karl Barlow looks like Nosferatu's big brother, all parchment skin and hairless pate, beady eyes, and bogeyman demeanor. Louis de Pointe du Lac looks more like the young Johnny Depp: midnight dark and matinee handsome, a portrait of manners, grace, and bearing. It was a look that Christopher Lee could have personified had he started playing Dracula in his early twenties as opposed to his late thirties; or Klaus Kinski (another great Nosferatu, of course) if Herzog had recruited him fifteen years sooner, around the time of *The Pleasure Girls*.

'Salem's Lot is set in uptight New England, all pinched lips and winter and whitewashed weathered clapboard. *Interview* rises from the swamps of Louisiana, from the fervent, furtive, and vivacious streets of New Orleans, a city so hip that even enunciating its name makes speakers sound like they have a stick up their ass. "Naawleans" is how the locals say it, and the locals get it right. The Big Easy. And while *'Salem's Lot* expounds upon the adventures of a writer hunting down an unpleasant truth (the story of the Marston House), *Interview* tells of an unpleasant truth (you mean vampires *exist*????) seeking out a writer to whom he can tell his tale.

Rice wrote the short story that grew into the interview in the late

1960s, developing it into a novel some four years later. Publishers were slow to grasp it; in a remarkable turnaround, she had sold the movie rights (to Paramount) before she landed a book deal, and it is incredible now to think that the studio sat on the story for ten years before finally admitting they weren't going to do anything with it and letting the rights return to Rice. (Lorimar, its next owners, were similarly sluggish; it was the early 1990s before a movie mogul, David Geffen, finally bought the rights *and* made a movie, about which we will say no more.)

It is Dupont's story, then, but the name that everybody remembers from the book is Lestat, the elder vampire who turned Louis back in 1791 while he worked on a Louisiana indigo plantation, and who then educated the young man in the ways of vampirism.

They move to New Orleans where they meet Claudia, a six-year-old girl whom Louis discovers dying of the plague, lying alongside the corpse of her mother. Louis feeds on her and leaves her for dead, only for Lestat to reanimate her as a vampire, an act that horrifies his protégé and ignites his rebellion. Together, Louis and Claudia scheme a life without Lestat, killing him (which, of course, is not as easy as they hoped) and then fleeing to Europe, where they hope to meet more of their own kind. But scouring Eastern Europe turns up nothing more than a bunch of animated corpses, so they head back west to settle in Paris.

There they encounter Armand, the four-century-old owner of one of the decadent city's most sinister attractions, the Théâtre des Vampires. And what a brilliant concept that is. Operating wholly in the light of day (figuratively speaking, anyway), the Théâtre specializes in vampire-themed stage shows, open both to the general public and any aspiring actor or actress who cares to audition.

It is so realistic too. Nightly, Paris society flocks to watch the denizens of the playhouse swoop down in their finest vampire regalia to feast upon unsuspecting humans, and so terrified are the screams, and so realistic the blood, that, *mon Dieu*, you could almost believe they really *were* vampires!

By now Louis and Claudia have new companions: Louis is growing ever closer to Armand, while Claudia has taken up with

Madeleine, a doll maker. This is when Lestat, with Rasputinlike tenacity, returns to the scene. He slaughters Claudia and Madeleine; Louis then destroys the Théâtre and almost all of its occupants before returning to the United States—to New Orleans—to tell his story. Which he clearly made sound a lot more glamorous than he intended to. Louis expected the young journalist, Thomas, to be repulsed. Instead he is intrigued, and begs Louis to turn *him* into a vampire. Louis refuses.

If you haven't read *Interview with the Vampire*, you should. (Charlaine Harris is herself a confirmed fan.) If you have, then reread it. It is a phenomenal story, but more than that, it follows the King custom of making the reader actively care about the characters, regardless of their vampiric tendencies. Indeed, that may well be the book's greatest achievement: that it seduces the reader into romancing the vampire, as opposed to merely painting him as the villain that some stake-bearing do-gooder will eventually get round to nailing.

Of course past writers, both in print and on film, had allowed the vampire to take center stage in the narrative, but the appeal was almost always as an antihero, the villain we love to hate. Here, Louis does not even feel like a villain; his own dreams and motivations spill out just as a human protagonist's would, and we identify with his needs and emotions just as readily we would any other great novel's lead character.

And having accomplished this—having proven to the reader that vamps have feelings too, as it were—Rice settled in for the long haul. Eventually. It took close to ten years for her to publish a sequel, with Lestat the focal point of 1985's *The Vampire Lestat*. After which *The Queen of the Damned* (1988), *The Tale of the Body Thief* (1992), *Memnoch the Devil* (1995), *The Vampire Armand* (1998), *Merrick* (2000), *Blood and Gold* (2001), *Blackwood Farm* (2002), and *Blood Canticle* (2003) continued the series now known as the Vampire Chronicles.

A second series, set within what modern comic-book parlance might term the same "universe," followed, called Lives of the Mayfair Witches; a brief third, New Tales of the Vampires, offered up *Pandora* (1998) and *Vittorio the Vampire* (1999). And one might want to argue that, just perhaps, the whole concept seriously ran out of steam some time before 2003, and serious health problems, brought an apparent end to the cycle.

Certainly none of the books that followed could even begin to enjoy the impact of *Interview with the Vampire*, not only on the reader but on popular culture in general. *'Salem's Lot* rehabilitated the vampire as a viable literary commodity; *Interview* lifted him out of literature and into the popular imagination. And everything after that was more or less icing.

Nevertheless, the gothic scene that developed as a primarily musical movement in the UK in the early 1980s, before exploding into a full-fledged cultural phenomenon a decade later, invariably drew its own stylistic and romantic impulses from Rice, as Rozz Williams, front man with America's finest-ever goth band, Christian Death, explained in a 1993 interview.

"Anne Rice either wrote, or revived, every cliché that the gothic lifestyle ever used." Jokingly, he outlined the sheer dedication that adherence to that lifestyle demanded: "It's kind of baffling. How do these people maintain it? Wake up, 'have to put in my fangs, do my hair.... Got to make it down to the graveyard before it's closed.' It really gets bad when people get stuck just in that, where they can't go outside of that. Where it's so strict with so many rules."

Absinthe, clove cigarettes, Victorian formal wear, codified beyond the demands of any past youth fashion (for of course, a lifestyle demands such vigor)—Rice did not necessarily invent the vampire's love of such things, but she did unite them, and Williams made another observation on that same theme. "Whenever I meet fans who term themselves goths, their names and appearances are always taken either from Anne Rice or Bram Stoker. I have *never* met anyone who wants to be Barlow."

THE RENQUIST QUARTET—MICK FARREN (1996–2002)

Having rejected science-fiction-themed vampirism a few chapters back, it is now time to turn that prohibition on its head by introducing you to Victor Renquist, a thousand-year-old nosferatu (he hates the term *vampire*) who can trace his lineage back to the lamia of Greek myth (see chapter 1). Author Mick Farren explains, "Renquist is very definitely something other than human, and I take the position that the supernatural is merely an advanced form of science that we have yet to understand.

"I nail him totally to the kind of crypto-history that claims aliens took control of Earth about 12,000 years ago, at the end of the last Ice Age; conducted genetic experiments on Cro-Magnon primates to create modern man; and also erected huge stone structures. [The aliens were also the biblical Nephilim from the Book of Enoch.] I also made the transformation of a human into a nosferatu a very complicated ritual, to avoid Matheson's *I Am Legend* paradox where each victim becomes a fresh vampire and they multiply exponentially until there are no people left."

It is this streamlining of the mythos that raises the four books in the quartet above so many other attempts to create a new vampiric paradigm—that and the fact that, above all else, vampires are fun! Well, Farren's are, anyway. "My first attraction to vampires is fairly basic. They live by night, have a wardrobe of really cool black clothes, and—most important—they don't have to die. It's all very teenage and really enjoyable."

The Time of Feasting (1996), *Darklost* (2000), *More Than Mortal* (2001), and *Underland* (2002) are the stories that make up the quartet, and every step of the way, Farren allows his own literary and historical fascinations to dictate the story, as opposed to any conventional rules of vampish lit.

"In the beginning I wanted Renquist to be a thousand years old, just because it had a kinda flourish to it. That took me to the eleventh century and the historical era of homicidal mass butchers like Simon de Montfort, and Pope Innocent III, and their brutal extermination of heretical sects like the Cathars. All that bloody 'Kill them all and let God sort them out' stuff. It seemed like a great place to start and that the Cathars should be sheltering Lamia, the female demon of Greek mythology—and that she is in fact a super ancient vampire—it seemed a cool way to get Renquist transformed to a nosferatu and started on his adventures."

The upshot, Farren continues, is a vampire who "probably owes more to James Bond and Michael Corleone than Dracula. I made him a proactive character, familiar with the paranormal [in the same way as] Dr. Strange, Doctor Who, or The Shadow. He leans towards human intrigue, conspiracy, and espionage.

"He was a favorite of Francis Walsingham, Elizabeth I's spymaster, and various Borgias and Medicis. Renquist and the other nosferatu in the stories tend to gravitate to less 'regular' humans— shadow government conspiracies, weird religious cults, dips into the Lovecraft mythos, Nazis in the hollow Earth with flying saucers; again with the crypto-history. He hung around St. Petersburg when he knew it was the time for change. He was in Osaka in the time of the Shogunates.... He also sees himself (increasingly so as the books progress) as a protector of mankind."

But not in a benevolent, selfish manner. He is more akin, Farren concludes ominously, to "a shepherd protecting his food supply."

The Mrs. Radcliffe of the bloodless horde, Nico was a German actress and model who just happened to make some of the most chilling music of the 1970s. (Roxie Releasing/Photofest)

7

TANZ DER BLOODSUCKERS: OR, AN IPOD FULL OF FANGS (PART 2)

Chapter 3 tells how gothic developed: how it was formulated and the multiple, manifold menaces from which it sent its tendrils slithering. Some went into art, some into literature, some into architecture. And a few went into music, to create what we now call gothic rock. At which point, we throw away everything we have already learned and begin again.

To trace gothic as a musical form back to any or all of these precedents is a waste of breath. Ian Astbury, vocalist with the band the Cult, was no more aware of Rosa when he took "The Witch" for an early 1990s song title than Adam Ant was of Harrison Ainsworth when he conjured his dandy highwayman from the pages of *Rookwood*.

True, any youth schooled and growing up in 1960s/'70s Britain could not help but be aware of the gothic heritage that pocks the landscape, from the novels of Sir Walter Scott to the crumbling walls of the Victorian follies that were the delight of eccentric aristocrats when they came to beautify their gardens. But the gothic with which we are concerned here was born of parents of considerably more recent vintage.

Sketching the story of gothic rock in his economically titled 1991 book *Gothic Rock*, author Mick Mercer dated the movement's genesis to just three bands, all operating in the UK at the turn of the 1970s: Bauhaus, Theatre of Hate, and Killing Joke. "But … it was what came after that was the fun, rough and tumble of it all—all in the shadow, wake or under the protective wing of UK Decay—Sex

Gang [Children], Ritual, Danse Society, Ausgang, Specimen, Alien Sex Fiend, Christian Death...all irresistibly different bands."

Maybe that's what is so special about it, that within so narrowly closeted a musical form, working from so few specific motives and modes, there was so much variety and so much theater. But it did not emerge from a void. There were precedents.

"DRACULA'S DAUGHTER"—SCREAMING LORD SUTCH (1964)

Thunder crashes, wind and rain roar, and an ear-splitting scream slits the moonlit night. A young man is passing the cemetery; the night is dark and the weather is foul. Feeling weak after a bite on his cheek, he meets "Vampire Mary."

Screaming Lord Sutch was never one to shroud his love of cheap horror movies. Though he certainly borrowed much of his early act (and his stage name) from the American Screamin' Jay Hawkins, the erstwhile David Sutch swiftly grew to eschew his role model's reliance on horror shtick as simply a visual device, and incorporated it wholly into his music as well, creating an absolute archetype as he did so.

A string of fabulous singles cut in the pre-Beatles age was his calling card. The creaking, moaning, howling "'Til the Following Night," produced by maverick producer Joe Meek, brought the banshee baron to life in 1961—the ghost of the Funeral March tapped out on a barely in-tune piano, a cacophony of agonized bellows and roars, and then the creature emerges, with horns on his head and a twinkle in his eye, and away to the dance club he twists, a rock 'n' rolling monster man until dawn breaks over the landscape and he returns to his coffin—'til the following night.

"She's Fallen in Love with the Monster Man" was next, an innocent dude taking his girl to the pictures and watching in dismay as she grabs an instant infatuation with the movie's hero. And why? Because she turns out to be Dracula's sister!

All his early records are excellent, but "Dracula's Daughter" was the best, Sutch in extremis, madcap rockabilly, and a silver-screen lyricism that distills every vampire seduction ever filmed and every undead lover ever pictured: "Lips of blue, eyes of red, a laugh like gurgling water ... I'm in love with Dracula's daughter."

The early 1960s were the heyday of the Hammer horror movie studios, themselves a quintessentially English definition of horror, and their reliance on, indeed, monster men and Dracula's family certainly influenced Sutch's own subject matter. His invocation of Jack the Ripper in 1963 was even more to the point—the girly chorus heralds Jack as a hero of the highest order, even as Sutch's lyric pulls no punches with its documentation of his ghastly crimes. Other artists borrowed from cinema—the James Dean and Marlon Brando rebel roles were alive and well from Hamburg to Hackensack. But Sutch alone zeroed in on the British love of schlock shock and ghoulish gore, and translated it into an unequivocally teenaged medium.

Horror films, by definition, were slapped with a forbidding X certificate. Rock 'n' roll, in those innocent days before Parental Guidance stickers were hauled from America's proud Puritan past, needed only dodge past adult disapproval—which, of course, was the obstacle it had relied upon to begin with.

Although he never scored a significant hit single, Sutch's celebrity never wavered. As a political figure, leader of what ultimately became the Monster Loony Raving Party, his electoral antics swiftly became as notorious as his earlier stage shows. Hardly surprisingly, then, he used the same gift for publicity grabbing at what remains his best-known performance, an appearance at the London Rock 'n' Roll Revival Festival in 1972. Particularly once he discovered it was being filmed for a concert movie.

Sutch occupied little more than five of the movie's eighty-four minutes, but he packed a lifetime of showmanship into them regardless. A rocked-up funeral march heralded his arrival, a frocked and brand-bearing resurrection man awaiting the arrival of his next piece of meat, while four hot-panted nubiles bore a virgin-white coffin aloft.

Only when the coffin opened did the grave robber realize his mistake. Wrapped in fur and armed with a club, a vampiric Neanderthal with a homicidal bent, Sutch emerged to the strains of a ragged "'Til the Following Night," and when his assailant shot him, the monster attacked, beating and choking the grave robber to death, while the band beat the soundtrack behind him. The scene and song ended with Sutch triumphant, gloating over the corpse of his victim; then the editor's scissors sliced into action, and suddenly it was the closing number, a grinding "Jack the Ripper."

Again Sutch acted the part—black hat, black cloak, a surgeon's bag by his side. But one key lyric change is more crucial than most onlookers might ever have realized. On record, Jack reels off the names of his historical prey, Jack's acknowledged victims. Onstage, he was searching for new blood—staggering Frankenstein-like through darkened streets, "looking for ... Alice Cooper."

"THE BALLAD OF DWIGHT FRY"—ALICE COOPER (1970)

Like Sutch, Alice Cooper is an integral figure in the story of gothic rock. Unlike Sutch, that's all he is. Newly arrived on the mainstream British scene in 1972 ("School's Out," Cooper's maiden hit, was No. 1 the week of the Rock 'n' Roll Revival), the American group—the name applied to both band and front man—drew on much the same theatrical premise as Sutch, with the financial backing to do it a lot better. At different times throughout the early 1970s, the Cooper stage show incorporated a gallows, an electric chair, a living snake, and a box of dead babies. The best Sutch ever managed were a few blazing brands and a plywood casket.

Cooper was garish, gruesome, and in the eyes of a shocked establishment, utterly gratuitous. When "little Jimmy ate a pound of aspirin" in the song "Dead Babies," concerned watchdogs begged the country's impressionable youth not to try this at home. At least one teenaged suicide was laid at the Coopers' door (the youth in question hanged himself), and the threat of the group's summer 1972 visit to Britain brought on a surge of authoritarian outrage that reached into the halls of government, as attempts to ban the band from British stages even reached the House of Commons.

They failed, just as attempts to outlaw Sutch had failed almost exactly a decade before. Indeed, they were met with much the same response from the would-be beleaguered offender. In 1962, Sutch announced his intention of standing for Parliament at the next General Election. In 1972, Alice Cooper…well, he didn't quite go that far. But his next single did insist, "I wanna be elected."

Plus, Alice Cooper cut no less than three crucial albums, from which can be distilled one disc's worth of genuinely essential material—a statistic that stands in bitter contrast to Sutch's tally of six great singles, any one of which can be considered definitive.

From *Billion Dollar Babies* (1973), the last and least of that sequence, recorded at a time when the band's popularity had exploded as a worldwide phenomenon and was thus informed as much by accounting as art, "Sick Things" and "I Love the Dead," the national anthem of necrophilia, are Hall of Famers in terms of both subject matter and presentation.

Two albums earlier, *Killer* (1971) gave us "Halo of Flies," the aforementioned "Dead Babies," and "Killer" itself, epic performances whose use of atmosphere and dynamic represents the peak of the group's musical creativity. But it is that album's predecessor, *Love It to Death*, which is the real Killer Klown, as "Black Juju," "Second Coming," and the magnificent "Ballad of Dwight Fry" unfold with a psychosis that is all but believable.

"Dwight Fry" is not, after all, merely a musical tour de force (although it is certainly a wryly placed highlight in Tim Burton's *Dark Shadows* movie). It also unleashes some potent iconography. The real-life Frye (note the extra *e*) was a jobbing actor through the 1930s and early '40s, appearing in a succession of generally B-standard movies, best distinguished by sundry Universal Studios *Frankenstein* films. His fame—and the Cooper song—however, rest upon one pivotal role, his portrayal of the madman Renfield alongside Bela Lugosi's count in 1931's *Dracula*.

The themes of despair and alienation that drive the Cooper song are a clear-cut embodiment of the insect-eating Renfield's own state of mind, and while the lyric does take the occasional liberty with the established plot line (including a genuinely sinister insinuation of child molestation), it is a powerful commentary regardless—all the more so since it segues directly out of "Second

Coming," in which Jesus Christ learns of his return to Earth from a poster on a wall. The link between religious fervor and criminal insanity, an unspoken staple of gothic rock's own schizophrenic approach to organized Christianity, could not have been forged with more clarity.

Nor could "The Ballad of Dwight Fry" have been improved upon. Later Alice would be gorier, later Alice would be scarier. But Fry succeeds not from what he does but from what he threatens. The terror is in the tease; the thrill is in the unknown. You've seen one vampire, you've seen them all, but if all you've ever done is sit in the dark waiting for that first one to manifest itself, then maybe you won't feel so glib.

To truly succeed, gothic demands, in no particular order, anticipation, transgression, ruin (physical or mental, it matters not), death (ditto). It is a feeling of formless foreboding, of deepening dread, of looming menace, but it is also a sense of spectacular grandiosity in a landscape where grandiosity should have no place; a flat, barren landscape punctured by a single, soaring tower; a mighty castle rising from the featureless fog; a single figure standing in the glow of a street lamp.

Which is precisely what it became.

RAVES FROM THE GRAVE—
TEN GREAT VAMPIRE ROCKERS

Bad Brains—"Fearless Vampire Killers" (from the album *Bad Brains*, 1982)

Blue Öyster Cult—"Nosferatu" (from the album *Spectres*, 1977)

Roky Erickson—"Night of the Vampire" (from the album *The Evil One*, 1981)

Hot Blood—"Soul Dracula" (and indeed, the rest of the *Disco Dracula* album, 1977)

The Misfits—"Vampira" (from the album *Walk Among Us*, 1982)

Harry Nilsson—"Daybreak" (from the soundtrack album *Son of Dracula*, 1974)

Ian North—"Vampire" (from the album *My Girlfriend's Dead*, 1980)

OutKast—"Dracula's Wedding" (from the album *Speakerboxxx/The Love Below*, 2003)

Rocket from the Crypt—"I Drink Blood" (from the various-artists album *Halloween Hootenanny*, 1998)

Neil Young—"Vampire Blues" (from the album *On the Beach*, 1974)

THE END—NICO (1974)

Nico, insists Bauhaus's Peter Murphy, recorded the first true gothic-rock album. Hotfoot from the Velvet Underground, the band whose frontline she shared with Lou Reed, Nico had already cut one solo album when she returned to the studio in 1968, and she really didn't like it. *Chelsea Girl* was all flutes and folkiness, sweet songs and sad sensations, against which the German-born actress/model/singer's naturally stentorian vocal stood out like a meat hook at a baby shower.

The Marble Index was the sound that Nico heard in her head, an icy wash of harmonium and wind, desolate and dark, with Nico herself the black queen presiding over a landscape blasted as barren as Narnia when the wardrobe first disgorges those meddling kids.

Neither was it a one-off. Record contracts were not easy for Nico to come by—over the course of the next twenty years, until her death in a bicycling accident in Spain, she released just four further albums: *Desertshore* (1971), *The End* (1974), *The Drama of Exile* (1980), and *Camera Obscura* (1985). All four are great, and the last two almost rock. But it is the first pair that you need to witness, as they pare the isolation of *The Marble Index* down to the bone and then keep on scraping.

The End is the starkest, darkest, and scariest; *The End* is the album that confirmed Nico's status as the Mrs. Radcliffe of the bloodless horde. A casket full of unrelenting howling gloom, with John Cale and Eno making noises round the edges, it was titled for the Doors' epic masterpiece of Oedipal rage, "The End," and in grasping the sheer nightmare of the lyric, Nico's version makes the original sound like a happy dance.

The End is terrifying on vinyl. Live, it was even bleaker. When Nico performed its highlights at an outdoor concert in London's Hyde Park in summer 1974, the surrounding trees turned to stone. And when she performed it again at Rheims Cathedral just before Christmas that same year, the Catholic Church demanded the building be reconsecrated.

A live recording of that performance was released in 2012, and while the sound quality is not all it could be, still the eleven songs are the soundtrack to every night you have ever spent sitting in the dark, waiting for the shadows on the wall to take solid form, waiting for your life to gutter like the candles.

The cathedral was draped in candles that night, and the darkness hung around them like the forces of evil, marshaling their strength in the building's natural resonance as it ricocheted Nico's voice from the old stone walls. She embraced the ancient confines of the cathedral as though it were a shroud, and it was with "Valley of the Kings," *The End*'s stately invocation of ancient Egyptian magic and mystery, that the chills first started to rise on the audience's arms.

"The End," drawn out to close to ten minutes and punctuated by a scream unheard since the height of the Inquisition, sent the temperature plummeting even further; legend, propagated by the church's own authorities, insists that the audience spent much of the evening copulating and urinating in the aisles of the cathedral. One would defy *anybody* to have dared even move a muscle as the performance wore on. Because to move would have invited attention, and who knew what unknown terrors clung to the pillars and walls, waiting to strike the unwary?

Spellbinding performances from a spellbinding performer, both *The End* and the Rheims Cathedral show are essential listening for anyone who has read this far, with the 2012 reissue of the studio record remastered to give the echoes even more space in which the specters can cavort. Nico herself died in 1988, but immortality never decays.

"O-RHESUS NEGATIVE"—UDO LINDENBERG (1975)

One of the longest-running success stories in the history of German rock, Udo Lindenberg was still close to the dawn of his career when he cut "O-Rhesus Negative," the not-too-sinister story of "a scary man with a large hat" accosting passers-by to inquire about their blood type. The title names the one that he dislikes most of all.

Performed in German (on Lindenberg's 1975 *Votan Wahnwitz* LP), it's a lighthearted number, detailing the idyllic life of the average vampire, sleeping all day, drinking all night. But a warning, too, that it is not as easy to become a vamp as some people might have you believe. For a start, you need a certificate from your dentist, because you won't get into their club … if your teeth are too short.

DAMNED DAMNED DAMNED—THE DAMNED (1977)

Not every great Dracula made it onto the silver screen. Not every great Dracula even saw himself as playing the role. But in the annals of pop culture's flirtations with the count, one name stands out for living the role without even appearing to try. A former gravedigger who had long since undertaken no longer to undertake for a living, the erstwhile David Letts was the singer with the Damned, one of the handful of bands that rose fully formed at the outset of the British punk rock movement, but whose musical lineage reached back to Alice Cooper and Screaming Lord Sutch.

It would be a decade more before Anne Rice pushed her vampire Lestat to the forefront of a rock band, by which time even her supporters were looking back at photos of Letts in his finest and wondering whether the pair might be related.

Offstage and on, Letts dressed the part, and he renamed himself accordingly; modeling himself after any of Dracula's suavest depictions, Dave Vanian was the archetypal Transyl-*vanian*. It is testament to his talent for self-perpetuation that, after more than thirty-five years in a similar role, he has become as much of an icon as his idol.

Throughout the Damned's long history (the band still plays on today), little of Vanian's night-stalker persona has been echoed in the band's music, although one cut on their debut album, "Feel the Pain," has a certain Alice Cooper vibe in tow. This may be a disappointing development for the vicarious onlooker, but with hindsight, it is an extraordinarily wise one. To obsess on Vanian's appearance, after all, would have been to flag it as something that the band themselves found remarkable, like pinning a placard to the village idiot. To the Damned, as founder member Brian James recalled, "What would have been the point of dwelling on it? It was just who Dave was. We might as well have written a song about my leather jacket." And the fact that half of the Damned's audience was indeed wearing leather jackets only backs up his remarks. Because the other half was dressed up like Vanian.

"Long before there was a recognized gothic look," James continued, "there were fans turning up at shows dressed like Dave, which was brilliant at the time, because it lifted us right out of the typical punk rock band thing. Other groups had the safety pins and the spitting and the bondage trousers, but you went to a Damned show, and half the local cemetery would be propped up against the stage."

Drummer Rat Scabies went on, "Dave's whole thing, right from the start, had been that he was a kind of vampire bloke. It wasn't something he put on just before he went onstage, it was the way he was when he got up in the morning, went to bed, working on the car. He was committed to that look…and that's why we stuck with him, because people would say, 'Ah, look at him, he's funny'; but he really wasn't. He was probably the most genuine person [in the band]."

"BELA LUGOSI'S DEAD"—BAUHAUS (1979)

Just one of the myriad bands formed in the UK in the aftermath of the 1976–1977 punk rock explosion, Bauhaus were based in the decidedly unpunky midlands town of Northampton—an upbringing they shared with comics author Alan (*V for Vendetta*) Moore.

Intrigued by art as much as music, and originally visualizing their breakthrough coming through an ambitious video project, the band scaled back only when financing and technology proved beyond their grasp. Instead, they booked themselves into the tiny Beck Studios in nearby Wellingborough, there to record a demo tape comprising five songs—or rather, four songs and a legend.

"Boys," "Dark Entries," "Some Faces," and "Harry" were all distinctive enough, in an adrenalined, savage-y kind of way. But then there was "Bela Lugosi's Dead," an extended opus that wasn't simply unlike anything else on the tape. It was unlike anything else, period.

They recorded it live in one take because none of them had a clue how to do anything else, and when the studio owner first heard what they were trying to do, he stood back as well. Their vision was so peculiar, and so unique, that only they could determine whether or not it was working out as they expected. So he set up the best sound he could, showed guitarist Daniel Ash and bassist David J. how to operate the sound effects, and left them to get on with it. A little under ten minutes of scratching, clicking, scraping, and yowling later, it was all finished.

Ash and J. set the song in motion—Ash by slowing down an old Gary Glitter glam-rock riff and then torturing the chords, J. by inventing a chorus that asked that most essential of questions: how could Bela Lugosi be dead, when his life was spent playing the greatest of the undead? And singer Peter Murphy still recalls the day he got a call from Ash telling him about the song. "I received a telephoned 'Hey Pete! Dave's got this lyric to this song and it's called "Bela Lugosi's Dead."'" And I said, 'What? Bela Luigi Who?' And he was 'No, no … Bela Lugosi.'"

Even on paper, with no lyric outside of that initial, half-formed chorus, "Bela Lugosi's Dead" was dynamic. It tiptoed in on nothing more than percussion, a rattlesome, window-tapping rhythm into which a descending three-note bass line almost unwillingly inserted itself. Then the guitars started scratching, echoing around the vault, and the curtain had yet to rise. Murphy had yet to open his mouth.

The lyric takes an age to arrive, a bat- and blood-soaked verse that draws every prop from Bela's bag of tricks, all intoned in a suitably sepulchral moan that itself sounds like the timeless howl of an ageless fiend.

It was relentless, one of those so-rare moments when performer and performance, mood and music, are so exquisitely united that the raw ingredients themselves are lost. Either that or transformed.

Guitars became the creaking of a dry and dusty coffin lid. The bass was hollow footsteps sounding in a deserted corridor above your head. The drums were the flapping of an army of bats, and Murphy—Murphy was the count, dead, undead.

The lyric, Murphy explains, sprang from a conversation between the band members one night, concerning "the erotic quality of vampire movies, even if they were the Hammer horror type. There was this conversation about the sexuality and eroticism of Dracula, and how that was very, very powerful for a pubescent male...or female. Never mind the form of what we look at now as being kitsch Hammer Horror movies—to our minds, relatively, they were *real* horror movies. But they have this underlying immorality and twisted religious-osity and, therefore, really related well with a pubescent glamorous eroticism."

Bauhaus's achievement was not simply a musical victory, however. "Bela Lugosi's Dead" would swiftly come to stand as a cultural watershed, too, the moment when themes that had long flourished within the realms of rock 'n' roll gimmickry (from "Monster Mash" to the Cramps, from Screaming Jay Hawkins to primal Alice Cooper) finally stepped out of the novelty circus and into something approaching legitimate art. That Bauhaus were merely just one more in a long line of contenders, any of whom *could* have sparked the gothic rock movement that emerged in Bela's wake, is beside the point. Any of them could have done it. But Bauhaus did it.

Their secret was their aforementioned comprehension of the erotic element. Other rockers, again, had played with Dracula and, indeed, other horror staples, but they had done so from an angle predicated in the comedic possibilities of the genre. Bauhaus adopted the opposite approach; if anything, Murphy later confessed, they took it *too* seriously. Or allowed their audience to do so, which amounts to much the same thing.

"'Bela Lugosi's Dead' was a very tongue-in-cheek song, which sounds extremely serious, very heavyweight and quite dark. But the essence of the song, if you peel back the first layer, is very tongue-in-cheek, 'Bela Lugosi's dead, undead'—it's hilarious.

"Look at the cover of 'Bela,' which is a still from pure Gothic cinema, *The Cabinet of Dr. Caligari*. That was the aesthetic we identified with a lot, although it wasn't on an academic level, it was that relativity of the songs and also what we looked like. I looked at stills of *Dr. Caligari*, having never seen the film, and I said, 'That's me, that's what I look like.' After the fact. I looked like this somnambulant character without knowing he existed, so it wasn't a mask or an emulation or anything, that's what we were.

"The mistake we made is that we performed the song with such naive seriousness! That's what pushed the audience into seeing it as a much more serious thing. The intense intention going into the performance actually overshadowed the humour of it."

"MARTIN"—SOFT CELL (1983)

Director George A. Romero has described it as his favorite out of all his movies, and you would probably need to be a zombie not to agree. Released in 1978, *Martin* (a.k.a. *Martin the Blood Lover*) may, as the movie posters insisted, be "the boy next door." He may have a good job, delivery boy for his cousin Tateh Cuda's butcher's store. He may even be so well behaved that some folk describe him as being almost old-fashioned.

But he is also a brutal killer, and the first time we see him, which is the opening scene of the movie himself, he is riding an overnight train and stabbing a sleeping girl with a syringe full of narcotics. Then he slashes open her wrist with a razor blade and raises the wound to his lips. Who says railroad food is all bad?

Soft Cell were an English electronic duo that scored a massive worldwide No. 1 hit in 1981 with the burbling, blinking "Tainted Love," a deceptively poppy performance that disguised the almost maggoty rancour that was frontman Marc Almond and keyboard player Dave Ball's traditional outlook on life. Their best songs were their sleaziest. They soundtracked a life in the gutter that lies below the one that the average degenerate aspires toward: a world of cut-rate peepshows and bondage-dripping leather boys, where daylight is dampened beneath the glow of gaudy neon, where it doesn't matter what you are willing to pay for something; there is always someone who will make you pay more.

It is a world in which Martin would probably feel right at home, if only he could escape the cloying attentions of his cousin, an old man who is so convinced the boy is a vampire that the boy does not doubt it himself. Certainly his dreams are filled with monochromatic visions of vampiric cruelty, and persecution too, although none of the traditional tricks that the old man employs to slake or slay the vampire's thirst ever seem to work. Crucifixes, garlic, statues of saints—Martin shrugs them all away. And then he shrugs away his cousin and flees his hometown, Braddock, PA, for the bright lights of Pittsburgh, where he can feast unmolested.

Martin the movie asks more questions than it answers. We believe the boy to be a vampire because that is what his cousin tells him. But does he behave the way he does because he truly needs it to survive? Or because his cousin told him he did? The observation that he feels less of an impulse to kill for blood once he starts having regular sex with his neighbor Mrs. Santini is definitely one that should be pursued by the psychologically inclined, while Marc Almond's lyric leaves us in no doubt whatsoever that family history, an overactive imagination, and an unhealthy fixation with creepy movies play as great a role in the boy's behavior as anything else. "Martin needs his strange obsessions to exist." Which is of no help whatsoever at the end of the movie, as Tateh stakes the boy through the heart and buries him in the back garden, giving final, ghastly consummation of those strange obsessions of his own.

Martin the movie, like Martin the boy, did not enjoy a happy childhood. Premiered at Cannes in 1977, *Martin* was a 165-minute opus shot entirely in black and white. By the time it was released in 1978, however, it had been sliced down to what Romero regarded as a more manageable 95 minutes, with color and, for the European version, a new soundtrack by the Italian progressive rock band Goblin. Titled *Wampyr* (and very badly dubbed), this version lurks on the double-DVD version of *Martin* released in the UK in 2010. Of the original marathon, Romero insists no cut exists.

The song, however, confirms its immortality. Included as a bonus twelve-inch single within Soft Cell's second album, the immaculately titled *The Art of Falling Apart*, "Martin" itself is cinematic, a John Barry/James Barry overture looped beneath sledgehammer percussion, while Almond switches from a third-person discussion of Martin and his miseries to a deeply personalized personification of the tumult taking place in his mind, the torches in the trees and the insatiable lust for blood, the voices whispering "kill, kill, kill," and around them, other voices whispering, speaking, calling, imploring his name.

The song, like the movie, ends with another question. Onscreen, Martin is a regular contributor to a radio call-in show, where his confusions led to the host rechristening him "the count." The movie wraps with other listeners calling to demand to know "Where's the count?" The song concludes with an equally disembodied voice demanding to know where *Almond* is. The suggestion that Martin's sickness was contagious after all is suddenly inescapable.

We all have a very good idea how it is spread, as well.

He may not have been the original, but to many, he's the best. Bela Lugosi, decidedly undead. (Author's collection)

8

SHADOWS ON THE SILVER SCREEN: THE GREATEST DRACS OF ALL

Other vamps may be more attractive, others may be more impressive. But in the world of vampire moviedom, Dracula is, always has been, and doubtless forever will be the No. 1 box-office bloodsucker.

It took less than twenty-five years for Dracula to be translated from the printed page to moving pictures—a remarkable achievement when one considers that movies themselves were still in their very infancy when he first flapped his wings across a spellbound public. Now he is just under a decade short of celebrating his cinematic centennial (in 2021), a span within which he has exercised the thespian abilities of a small telephone directory's worth of actors and probably consumed his own weight in celluloid.

Not all of the movies and TV shows purporting to tell the (or even a) story of Count Dracula have been great; some, in fact, have been downright appalling. But the best of the best are ranked among some of the greatest movies ever made. Beginning with…

NOSFERATU, EINE SYMPHONIE DES GRAUENS (NOSFERATU: A SYMPHONY OF HORROR) (1922)

Friedrich Gustav Maximilian Schreck was born on September 6, 1879, and was just fifty-seven when he passed away on February 20, 1936. By that time, however, he had already grasped an immortality that remains unique in the annals of cinema—the first vampire ever to stalk the silver screen *and survive*.

That is an important distinction to make. *Nosferatu*, the 1922

German movie that established Schreck's reputation, is the oldest vampire film to be viewable today. But it was preceded by *Drakula Halála* (*Dracula's Death*), a 1921 Hungarian production in which Dracula (Paul Askonas) is being held in a lunatic asylum, and visiting him causes a young lady, Mary (Lene Myl), to suffer strange and disturbing hallucinations.

But the movie has long been lost, a fate that *Nosferatu*, too, came close to suffering. Attempts to license the rights to Bram Stoker's novel from his estate having proven fruitless, the newly launched Prana Films studio went ahead and made their planned movie anyway, hoping that changing a few key names (Dracula became Count Orlok), locations, and situations would deflect any suspicious inspections.

It didn't. No matter that the story was now set in Germany and omitted any mention of a Van Helsing–style character, nor that Orlok operated under the shadow of a plague that had accompanied him to his new hunting grounds, allowing its ravages to take the blame for his own killings. Still *Nosferatu* was more or less sued into extinction, with every known copy of the print destroyed as part of the settlement with Stoker's aggrieved widow.

Every *known* copy. But like the lone vampire escaping at the conclusion of some gory B-movie flesh-fest, one copy miraculously survived, and it is from this single print that *Nosferatu* prospered and proliferated—carrying Max Schreck with it.

Ironically, Schreck was already accustomed to a life in the shadows. As a child in Berlin, his early inclination toward theater was fiercely opposed by his father. It was his mother who secretly provided him with the money that he needed to take acting lessons, a subterfuge that came to a close only after Schreck senior passed away and the boy could openly enroll in drama school.

Schreck graduated from his training at the State Theater of Berlin in 1902 and moved immediately into theater, eventually joining the famed Max Reinhardt's troupe of players. World War I interrupted his career, as he was called up to serve in the military, but he was back in his own world by the early 1920s. Schreck had a role in the first-ever production of a Bertolt Brecht play, *Drums in the Night*, and also made his first movie appearances.

Nosferatu initially seemed no more than a job of work for Schreck, with its sad and sudden death depriving the majority of people from seeing it, even at the time. What they missed, of course, was a master performance, not only from the ferociously made-up Schreck—all spindly limbs and terrifying glares, bald head, and bat ears—but from director F. W. Murnau too.

His use of shadow play is responsible for some of the most heart-stopping moments in a movie that, by the standards of the time, was genuinely terrifying, and he was clearly impressed by his star. Murnau and Schreck would work together again on 1924's comedy *Die Finanzen des Großherzogs* (*The Grand Duke's Finances*); Schreck also appeared in Brecht's one-reel comedy *Mysterien eines Friseursalons* (*Mysteries of a Barber's Shop*) and was among that select handful of silent movie stars who effortlessly transcended the arrival of the talkies.

Theater remained his bread and butter, however; following his death from a heart attack in 1936, Schreck's obituaries dwelt more on his appearance as the Miser in Molière's play of the same name than any of his movie roles, and it would be many years before his Count Orlok was rediscovered by movie scholars and fans and proclaimed his true crowning glory.

And yet, rumors already persisted. Schreck's reputation was that of a loner, a man who not only preferred his own company offstage and offscreen but was also at his best in roles that repeated that isolation. He took long walks, it was said, in the darkest and most ominous locations he could find, and the world that he constructed around himself and his wife, Fanny, was one that friends and visiting journalists alike found strange, disquieting, disturbing.

What could have been more appropriate?

DRACULA (1931)

Bela Lugosi may not always be viewed as the greatest cinema vampire of all time, and he certainly wasn't the most attractive. But few of the actors and actresses who have portrayed a vampiric

IF YOU LIKE TRUE BLOOD...

role, particularly among those who have taken on the best-known of them all (go on, guess), have ever seen themselves as anything but one more soul following in the footsteps of the most legendary of them all.

Bela Blasko was born on October 20, 1882, in the Hungarian town of Lugos. His stage name was thus a variation on his hometown, adopted following his arrival in America in 1921, by which time he had already made a string of movies in both Hungary and Germany.

Close to forty years of age, his impact on his adopted homeland was negligible. He made his Hollywood debut in 1923's *The Silent Command*, but the talkies seemed set to murder him. His meager command of the English language saw him confined to mere bit parts, and even there he struggled. Any lines he was given, he learned phonetically, but worse was to come.

Having been hired to direct a drama, *The Right to Dream*, Lugosi was fired when it became embarrassingly obvious that he was incapable of even communicating with his cast. He sued for wrongful dismissal, but the court could make no more sense of his complaint than the actors could of his direction. He lost the case and was forced to auction off his own possessions to pay the legal fees.

Undeterred by such catastrophes, Lugosi remained on the fringes of the acting world, and in 1927, he was finally offered a role in which his heavily accented, beguilingly faltering English would play to his advantage, the title role in the Broadway adaptation of the smash hit London stage show *Dracula*. Appearing alongside Herbert Bunston (Dr. Seward), Bernard Jukes (Renfield), Dorothy Peterson (Lucy), and Edward Van Sloan (Van Helsing), Lugosi was an immediate sensation. He remained in the role for three years, then returned to Hollywood in triumph to repeat the feat on film.

Dracula was a new sensation for Americans. We have already seen how, a decade previously, Hungarian director Károly Lajthay had adapted *Dracula* for a moving picture. Tragically, his *Drakula* is long lost, but its success can be gauged from the fact that just a few months elapsed before Friedrich Murnau recast the story as

Nosferatu, while the London play (the first, incidentally, ever to win the approval of the Stoker estate) had been running since 1924. Now, finally, Broadway was thrilling to the vampire's embrace, and when *Dracula* became one of the most successful stage plays of the era, Hollywood too was ready to succumb to the same savage seduction.

Universal Studios, the movie's backers; and Tod Browning, the director, originally had no intention whatsoever of casting Bela Lugosi in the movie role, much preferring Lon Chaney Jr. He, however, was battling cancer at the time and was too ill to work. Other possibilities fell through. Finally, Lugosi was the only name left in the frame. He became Dracula—in every sense of the phrase.

It is impossible today to recapture the sheer power of *Dracula*. Again, vampire movies were new to American eyes and ears—had *Nosferatu* even been shown in this country before it was so rudely crucified? No, it hadn't. *Dracula*, however, rode the renown of the stage show to the top of the box office, then rode its own moody atmosphere and unparalleled scenes of horror and ugliness even further.

Overnight, Lugosi was reinvented from a litigious mumbler who once had an affair with Clara Bow to the hottest property in Hollywood, an international star who suddenly found he could take—or turn down—any role he chose.

It was a freedom in which he revelled to the full, although not necessarily to his own advantage. Among the subsequent movie offerings that he was offered, but rejected, was the title role in director James Whale's forthcoming *Frankenstein*, turning it down in favor of a role in another European masterpiece, a remake of *The Hunchback of Notre Dame*, titled for its main character, Quasimodo.

Unfortunately, while *Frankenstein* rocketed to peaks approaching *Dracula*'s own, *Quasimodo* was never made, and Lugosi—who had seen that role as essential to proving he was more than a simple stereotype monster—would never really recover. Although he remained constantly in demand, he was indeed stereotyped— if not as Dracula, then at least as a mysteriously sinister Eastern

European—and few of the movies he made throughout the remainder of his career ever allowed him to break out of that cliché. By 1948, Lugosi was reduced to caricaturing his finest moment in the comedy *Abbott and Costello Meet Frankenstein*, a depth that apparently horrified him so much that he would not return to the screen for another four years.

Lugosi's genius, albeit one that led directly to his downfall, was that he was so eminently believable. No matter that the count, as played by the Hungarian, was subsequently to become punishingly parodied, not only by Lugosi himself, but by countless other would-be bloodsuckers too. Throughout the 1930s, when a nervously isolationist America was spotting fresh foes under every bed, Lugosi's Dracula was flesh-eater made flesh. From the moment he first materializes in *Dracula* to that in which he is vanquished at the end, Lugosi not only overcomes any incredulity that his own audience might have felt toward the entire concept of Transylvanian bloodsuckers, but he also vanquishes that of any modern viewer. He was, quite simply, too damned brilliant for his own good.

Tiring of his exile, and with his bank account again in cobwebbed tatters, Lugosi resurfaced in 1952, finally forced to accept his fate by an appetite for drugs that demanded he take all the employment he was offered. And if the only work he could get was as a parody of himself, then he would be the greatest parody of them all. His every subsequent public appearance would find him clad in full costume, while the films he now made were purposefully calculated to play on his reputation: *Bela Lugosi Meets a Brooklyn Gorilla*, *My Son the Vampire*, *Old Mother Riley Meets the Vampire*, and a pair of films with the eccentric Ed Wood, *Glen or Glenda?* and *Bride of the Monster*.

All kept the wolf from the door, but they weren't enough. In 1955, Lugosi voluntarily committed himself in the hope of shaking off his dope habit. He succeeded, but at a dreadful cost. Having shot just a handful of scenes for another Wood spectacular, *Plan 9 from Outer Space*, Lugosi was felled by a massive heart attack. On August 15, 1956, the world learned that Bela Lugosi, as the song later reminded us, was dead.

THE VAMPED-OUT UNIVERSE OF EDWARD GOREY

S wooning maidens, mysterious demises, addled madmen, and ax-murdering fiends—the opening credits to PBS's *Masterpiece Mystery!* ... and a series of tiny books that have captivated audiences for over half a century.

This is the legacy of Edward Gorey (1925–2000), the Chicago-born artist whose exquisite drawings and twisted lyricism brought us some of supernatural fiction's best-loved characters—the fiendish Figbash, the wicked Wuggly Ump, numerous alligators, and best of all, Sarah Jane (Batears) Olafsen, the mild-mannered serial killeress who "hacked to collops nineteen loggers" in the back woods of turn-of-the-century Oregon.

The *New York Times* once described him as having been "born to be posthumous ... the master of high-camp macabre," and if any artist can be said to have utterly inverted the values of the age in which he lived, it was Gorey. Like Charles Addams, whose Addams family thrived through much of the same era, Gorey's work started out with a vision of normalcy, then sent it twisting down avenues of his own imagination. Unlike Addams, Gorey was never tied down to just the one set of characters. His world may have been rooted in the visual values of Victoriana; his women might seem to have stepped out of the auditions that brought Irma Vep, star of the 1915 French crime movie *Les Vampyres* (concerning vamps, not vampires), to silent movie fame. But his characters were drawn from all walks of life and death ... and the more bizarre and sudden that death, the better.

His bats, all apparently caught in the instant before they transform into vampires, are among his best-loved creations—they have even been marketed as cuddly toys! And when *Dracula* visited the Broadway stage in 1977, reviving the original 1920s production that brought Bela Lugosi to fame (Frank Langella took the title role), it was to Gorey that the producers turned for set design. He rewarded them with a set that was nominated for a Tony Award, and which was all the more effective for its apparent whimsy.

Elsewhere in his canon, intricately cross-hatched gazebos and mausoleums pock the landscape, each one resplendent with precariously balanced urns. Storms whip the world, and unfathomable evil arises from the most innocuous surroundings; a night spent leafing through Gorey's work, best collected in the three-volume anthology *Amphigorey*, is to fast-forward through a history of human horror shattered through a prism of the blackest humor, the most livid lunacy, and some of the most reassuringly ridiculous ends that any poor soul could embrace. "Gorey's images," says author and Gorey authority Amy Hanson, "do not go lightly into the realms of forgotten memory. They stick, and they stick well."

THE BODY BENEATH (1970)

The Reverend Alexander Algernon Ford is rarely, if ever, cited among cinema's most memorable vampires. But an evening in the company of American-born, London-based director Andy Milligan's *The Body Beneath* will reveal that it is the movie's subsequent obscurity that cloaked his qualities, as opposed to any deficiency in his performance or demeanor.

Quite simply, the Reverend is as megalomaniacal, twisted, and single-minded as any better-known vampire king could be, and the fact that the movie is not anywhere close to being as well known as the grindhouse material Mulligan went on to make is, perhaps, a greater loss than the survival of his other work is a benefit. *Bloodthirsty Butchers*, *Torture Dungeon*, *The Man with Two Heads* . . . these are the movies for which Milligan is renowned. But the Rev was a stronger creation than any of them.

The Body Beneath was Milligan's second supernatural opus (following the now-lost 1967 film *The Naked Witch*), and it deliberately tapped into the self-same terrors, at the exact same time, that were discussed in this book's introduction: the existence of a vampire of Highgate Cemetery—or, in Milligan's mind, an entire dynasty of them. It is there, in the beautifully unkempt, prerestoration tangle of the cemetery, that the movie begins, with a brief sequence of a young woman visiting her mother's grave, there to be welcomed by three sinister, blue-faced, and certainly fatale femmes.

An obsequious priest (Gavin Reed), a well-intentioned Graham Ford (Colin Gordon), and what would have been considered a very steamy lovemaking scene for his sister Susan (Jacqueline Skarvellis) and her boyfriend return the movie to the here and now, with even the vampires' victim (who turns out to be Graham's wife, Anna) seemingly unaffected by her experience.

But slowly the mood changes. Opening the front door to accept a floral delivery, the Fords' maid admits one of the three creatures from the graveyard, and now we see the priest for who he is, the magnificently named Reverend Alexander Algernon Ford (yes, they are all related) binding together the disparate strings of his vampiric cult, quaffing what he claims to be tomato juice, and complaining about having to move around by day. "But I suppose somebody has to."

Reed's performance is startling. He could have been an ultracamp comic, and does in fact take on that kind of role in Dustin Hoffman's 1982 movie *Tootsie*, where he plays a bullying theater director. But *The Body Beneath* is not played for laughs, and the Reverend is the epitome of upper-class superficiality: so polite to your face but beneath the facade, a seething cauldron of evil and loathing.

Elements of *Rosemary's Baby* are borrowed for the Reverend's plot but are taken in a very different direction. To paint his vampires as simply a race of baby snatchers, however, is to overlook all the other aspects of his unfolding master plan, working toward the restoration of his family to the power that it once was, before the gene pool was diluted by "outsiders," and kidnapping all the relatives he can find so that he might test the strength of their blood. Then it will be off to America with the lot of them, there to breed again in fresh seclusion.

Milligan's vampires are both classic and unique. Sunlight merely weakens them, but they have no reflection; religious iconography does not bother them in the slightest, but they revel in gothic chic (the Reverend's lair, Carfax Abbey, could have been a Victorian show home). He employs a simpleminded hunchback servant named Spool (Berwick Kaler), but treats him more as a regular gopher. He employs his own wife to do his dirty work— slaying a disobedient maid with her knitting needles is an especially gruesome touch.

Then there are his three blue-bodied brides, silently stalking whomever they fancy, garishly grinning beneath their blonde fright wigs. It is they who half-crucify Spool when he is discovered becoming too friendly with one of the Reverend's unwilling house guests, they who are dispatched to kill those family members in whom the Rev has no further interest.

All of which leads up to the movie's climax, twenty-one centuries' worth of former Fords raising themselves from their Highgate graves to participate in a garishly costumed, gorgeously choreographed, and nightmarishly soundtracked banquet; the final slaughter of Spool and the luckless living Fords; and then the shocking discovery that not all of the vampires fled the country after all. One pair got left behind.

BLACULA (1972)

As the repository for some of the sharpest assaults upon religious, sexual, racial, and political fundamentalism currently masquerading as popular entertainment, *True Blood* is very much a child of its times—times in which society has finally begun to frown upon, and even legislate against, the divisions that have always split the world in which we live. They still exist, of course. But no longer are there active, legal barriers against people deemed to be of the wrong color, creed, inclination, or race, and those that *do* still exist do so only in the face of rising popular opposition.

Fifty years ago, the very suggestion that a gay African American Wiccan could legally marry her white Christian lover and raise a family of adopted children would have induced apoplexy and worse in the pages of the popular press. We have by no means reached a place where such an arrangement will be unquestioningly accepted by *everyone*, but still we can watch the interspecies prejudice that underlies so much of *True Blood* and remember "the bad old days" when "everybody" felt that way.

Which is why it's very unlikely that anybody could get away any longer with creating a genre of movies under the overall banner of "blaxploitation," nor that such films would even be required any longer. Forty years ago, however, it was a very different world.

Sensing a vast hole in the Hollywood machine where actors and actresses of color should have slipped, a handful of enterprising early 1970s film makers took to producing movies that were staffed almost exclusively by African Americans, placing them in all the roles that had traditionally gone to hunky white leading men and women, and in the process creating some of the best action, Western, romance, and drama movies of the period.

Horror movies were especially notoriously low on black cast members, particularly those that did not require a handful of cannibals, witch doctors, or voodoo zombies. But then *Blacula* materialized (even the title makes the modern politically correct soul shiver a little), and all bets were off.

The movie opens with the true Dracula, carefully portrayed by Charles Macaulay, visiting Africa in 1815 and being approached by a local prince, Mamuwalde (William Marshall) and his wife Lyuka (Vonetta McGee), who hope the aristocratic European might sign a petition they are organizing, demanding the abolition of slavery. Drac doesn't sign. Instead he bites the pair, transforming them into vampires, and for good measure saddling the prince with what he, the count, regards as a very pejorative name. And 150-some years later, the pair are revived to wreak havoc on the streets of modern Los Angeles.

In that respect, *Blacula* is scarcely different from any of many other treatments of the modern vampire story. Blacula himself, however, is. William Marshall was a Shakespearean veteran best known to cinema audiences for his performance as the Nubian King Glycon in *Demetrius and the Gladiators* (the sequel to Victor Mature's Roman epic *The Robe*); he was also a first-hand victim of the very Hollywood system that ignited the blaxploitation boom in the first place. Having very successfully played the role of Henri Christophe, the first president of Haiti, onstage, Marshall should have been a shoo-in when it came to casting a movie of the same story. Instead the role went to Anthony Quinn.

Still fondly regarded on the cult circuit, *Blacula* was a phenomenal success upon release. Interviewed for Gerald and Diana Martinez's priceless examination of the blaxploitation boom, *What It Is … What It Was*, Marshall recalled "going to several movie houses and seeing … the reaction of African American audiences. You couldn't get them to leave, because they hadn't seen anything like this. Who had? And they were so delighted."

Marshall would return a year later in the equally riotous *Scream Blacula Scream*, this time with Pam Grier alongside him to confer her own superstar status upon the movie. And in a perfect world, there would have been plenty more follow-ups to come. Sadly, the golden age of blaxploitation was nearing its end, as Hollywood finally started to pay attention to the wealth of talent it had hitherto marginalized and, presumably, the wealth of profit it had overlooked. But yes, we do still await the next truly great black Dracula.

BLOOD FOR DRACULA (1974)

Lugosi's portrayal of Count Dracula is frequently proclaimed as the greatest there has ever been. But the competition is stiff, ranging as it does from the eternal Christopher Lee (see chapter 9) to the moody Frank Langella; from Max Schreck to the exquisite casting of British character actor Denholm Elliott in a 1968 UK television production; from Louis Jourdan to Thomas Kretschmann. And then there is Udo Kier, the titular star of one of the most divisive of all Dracula remakes, Andy Warhol's *Blood for Dracula* (1974).

Cursed to derive sustenance only from the blood of female virgins, Dracula decides that he is most likely to find a regular food source in a devoutly Catholic country. So he relocates to Italy, where he meets the Marchese di Fiore (Vittorio De Sica), a declining landowner who hopes to reverse his fading fortunes by marrying off one of his four daughters to a suitable aristocrat. He selects Dracula, but his assurances that all four of the girls are virgins turn out to be false. Dracula samples the two most attractive ones and finds himself becoming even sicklier. Things just get more bizarre from that point on.

Within the full canon of Dracula movies, *Blood for Dracula* is little more than an entertaining sideshow, a consequence perhaps of it having been conceived very much as an afterthought, financed by cash left over from another Warholian horror, *Flesh for Frankenstein*. But much the same can be said for many of the Dracula movies released during the early 1970s, especially once Hammer began placing formula over finesse, and under those conditions, *Blood for Dracula* can at least point to a novel plot and some finely charged performances.

Plus, it packs a cameo appearance from Roman Polanski (who was shooting in Italy at the same time), a brief onscreen moment that nevertheless establishes a firm line of descent from what is one of the greatest vampire movies of all, 1967's *The Fearless Vampire Killers, or Pardon Me, But Your Teeth Are in My Neck*.

BRAM STOKER'S DRACULA (1992)

One of the most sumptuous retellings of the old tale ever shot, Francis Ford Coppola's *Bram Stoker's Dracula* was also very much the truest cinematic interpretation yet of the original novel. It was one that fed through an almost flawless awareness of the legends that have since attached themselves to Dracula himself (not least of all his perceived descent from Vlad the Impaler) to become probably the ultimate study of the subject.

Writer James V. Hart's script was first brought to Coppola's attention by actress Winona Ryder, and the director recalled that his first question was, "Well, is it the real Bram Stoker's *Dracula*?" Coppola enthused, "She said, 'Yeah, yeah, yeah,' and when I read it, the first scenes are Vlad the Impaler, and I said, 'Oh, this is *real!*'" Indeed, the director continued, "I'm amazed, watching all the other Dracula films, how much they held back from what had been written or implied [in Stoker's book]. No one had ever done the book." Hart's screenplay "was closer to Stoker's novel than anything done before."

The project had enjoyed a convoluted genesis. Hart had spent thirteen years trying to place the script, but only recently had he found anybody willing to take a chance on it, aboard the USA cable TV network. A production of the script was already scheduled for the channel when Coppola weighed in and everything changed.

A deal was swiftly struck; Coppola would direct, Ryder would play Mina Harker, Jonathan Harker's bride-to-be and the apparent reincarnation of Dracula's long, long lost love. "I think Francis and I liked the same things about the script," Ryder explained at the time. "[It] was very romantic and sensual and epic. It's not really a vampire story; to me it's more about the man. Dracula, the warrior, the prince. He is unlike any other man. He's mysterious and very sexual, attractive in a dangerous way."

This, as Coppola has already pointed out, allowed the script to rest closer to Stoker's original than any other. Appending the author's name to the title of his greatest tale, as *Bram Stoker's Dracula*, allowed that proximity to be reinforced before a single sequence had been filmed. Yet that was not the reason why the movie wound up being called what it was. Far more mundanely, it was discovered that Universal Studios owned the rights to the unadorned *Dracula*. Stoker's name was affixed to preclude any accusations of copyright infringement.

There were other difficulties to surmount.

By the early 1990s, Dracula had been through every commercial wringer imaginable. His image had been invoked to sell everything from big-haired '80s pornography to the breakfast cereal Count Chocula. He had been turned into a rabbit, authors Deborah and James Howe's (admittedly charming) *Bunnicula* story, and invoked in soap opera (*Dark Shadows*' supremely cool Barnabas Collins). *The Munsters* and *The Addams Family* made sitcom light of his grandfatherly demeanor, and of course, every Halloween saw the drugstores overflow with Dracula fangs and flying bats. There was even a Muppet Dracula, who taught numeracy to children. His name was the Count.

But there is a reason for all that, and a very simple one, too. The critics may have considered Dracula to be a dried-up old property, but nobody else did. Not the people who bought the books, who watched the movies, who read the comics, who played the records, who lived the life. At the same time as Coppola was shrugging off everyone who doubted that even he could make a winner out of Drac, Anne Rice was gearing up for the fourth installment of her Vampire Chronicles series of novels, while a quick trip around the studios revealed that some half dozen other vampire movies were already either in, or approaching, production. Including: *Buffy the Vampire Slayer*, Roger Corman's *To Sleep with a Vampire*, and the already bordering-on-legendary first-ever adaptation of Rice's *Interview with the Vampire*. Not bad for a genre that nobody cared about.

While the critics chirruped their dour chorus, Coppola got on with the casting. Gary Oldman would play the title role, and watching the movie today, it is difficult to imagine anybody else even being considered. An Englishman whose past credits included biopics as disparate as Sid Vicious and JFK, he was widely regarded as an unconventional choice at the time, but he also proved the correct one. Nobody will ever displace Bela Lugosi as the King of the Counts. But Oldman came within an artery's width of equaling him.

Anthony Hopkins came aboard as the vampire hunter, Van Helsing; singer Tom Waits, a veteran of four Coppola movies (and two of Ryder's) was brilliantly cast as the luckless lunatic Renfield; and the only sour note was sounded by the inclusion of Keanu Reeves, the possibly overhyped star of *Bill and Ted's Excellent Adventure*, as Jonathan Harker. As more than one review either pointed out or insinuated, you could almost hear him saying, "Excellent fangs, Drac, dude."

Ryder's involvement, too, was questioned, the adolescent star of such past pinnacles as *Beetlejuice* and *Edward Scissorhands* suddenly placing such pursuits behind her to embrace her first so-called adult role. But she, too, came through with flying colors, and that despite a series of on-set flash points that so damaged her previously warm relationship with Coppola that she vowed never to work with the director again. She also made her way inadvertently onto a lot of people's favorite onscreen blooper reel with a very unconvincing portrayal of a corpse—a mishap that is so prominent that it seems impossible to believe nobody noticed it during filming and production and took the appropriate steps to address it.

All of this *could* have added up to create an absolute cinematic catastrophe. Instead, *Bram Stoker's Dracula* became one of the biggest hits of the year and, with its twentieth anniversary just past, one of the greatest realizations of the Dracula legend ever screened. It is beautiful, it is bloody, but most of all, it is believable—a combination not only of the stellar sets and gorgeous costuming, but also of Coppola's ability to truly wring the best out of his cast, whether they wanted it wrung or not.

SHADOW OF THE VAMPIRE (2000)

Just shy of the eightieth anniversary of *Nosferatu*, in 2000, director E. Elias Merhige, writer Steven Katz, and a cast that included Willem Dafoe, John Malkovich, and Udo Kier (who himself played the title role in 1974's *Blood for Dracula*) returned to the film set where that first movie was shot to ask: What if Schreck really *had* been a vampire? Playing himself on the silver screen and feeding his appetite on the real-life victims of his supposedly fictional depredations?

Shadow of the Vampire was not the first creation to posit such a scenario; fans of Anne Rice's Parisian vampiric theater will immediately see the similarities. But still, *Shadow of the Vampire* thrills, as Schreck (played with exquisite subtlety by Dafoe) chomps his way through the cast, growing increasingly uncontrollable as he gives director Murnau (Malkovich) exactly what he wanted, the most realistic vampire movie imaginable.

But the director does not flinch, capturing everything on film, and when the movie reaches its climax with the grotesque death of the vampire (together with most of the surviving cast), Murnau is as calm and unruffled as ever. "I think we have it all," he says as he shuts down the filming.

Shadow of the Vampire impresses not only through its plot. The movie itself is riddled with nods and homages to the original movie, including the use of intertitles to explain the action and that most glorious of all silent-movie techniques, the iris lens that enfolds a final screen within a circle of blackness.

And Max Schreck was reborn for a new century.

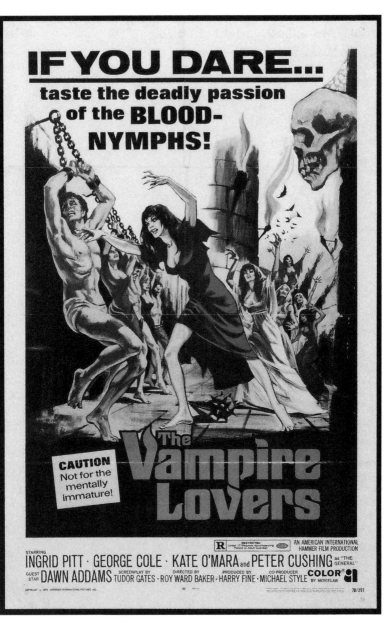

A true Hammer horror: *The Vampire Lovers* (1970) was the movie that made an icon of Ingrid Pitt. (Author's collection)

9

THE HORROR HAMMER: THE LITTLE BRITISH STUDIO THAT COULD

To the average British filmgoer of the 1940s and early 1950s, Hammer Films was one of those shoestring movie studios whose name really didn't mean much. It might register somewhere in the credits of a medium-maudlin B-picture—*Sporting Love* or *The Bank Messenger Mystery*, *Who Killed Van Loon?* or *We Do Believe in Ghosts*—but Hammer's hottest properties were the ones they borrowed from the radio, special agent *Dick Barton*, and policeman *PC 49*.

Radio dramas were exceedingly popular in those years before television was switched on across the UK, and putting faces and pictures to adventures that had hitherto existed only in audio was definitely a step in the right financial direction. So, it turned out, was making a big-screen version of a show that *had* been screened on TV but reached only a fraction of its potential audience because...well, because only a fraction of its potential audience had a TV.

The Quatermass Experiment, written by sci-fi author Nigel Kneale, was one of the television hits of 1953. Six episodes were broadcast, but they were filmed live and were never to be seen again—at the time, the BBC had no reliable method of recording its own output. Media coverage of the broadcast, however, was widespread and open armed; Quatermass, a grumpy scientist fixated on establishing Britain as the leader of the race into space, was widely proclaimed a new hero for the age, a resourceful near-genius who epitomized the country's own growing romance with technology. And he was not going to let any scary old alien invader ruin his plans.

If ever a TV show demanded an instant movie remake, it was *The Quatermass Experiment.* Or *X*periment, as Hammer retitled it once the British Board of Film Censors had decreed it could only be screened to over-eighteens, and saddled it with an X certificate.

It was huge. And brilliant. And so profitable that there was no way Hammer could allow the momentum to slip. *The Quatermass Xperiment* was hailed, and remains, one of the finest British horror movies ever, the tale of a deep-space mission that goes terribly wrong when the spacecraft returns and the one surviving crewman has been turned (or is on the point of turning) into a giant walking cactus. Which metamorphoses into an octopus. Which gets more and more pissed off with every passing moment. What Hammer needed now was to find an equally terrifying, equally dynamic successor.

The Curse of Frankenstein!

Followed by another Nigel Kneale script, *The Abominable Snowman*. Followed, with glee-streaked inevitability, by *Dracula*.

And while critics (and television reruns) today insist that Hammer films were deficient in every significant avenue of cinematic endeavor—acting, scripting, sets, plots, the lot—there was one area in which they were unimpeachable. Hammer films were scary. Maybe not in a sense that a modern audience would appreciate (although one must also question how much of modern horror is actually frightening and how much is simply sickening or gross); maybe not even in the way that a good ghost story, read by firelight on a windy winter's evening, can make one feel oddly susceptible to unexplained noises and a drop in the temperature. In terms of making you jump with a well-choreographed *Boo!*, however, Hammer banged the stake through your heart every time.

DRACULA (1958)

Hammer's inaugural *Dracula* movie is one of the greatest vampire films ever made. And Hammer's inaugural Dracula, actor Christopher Lee, is one of the greatest vampires. Tall, suave, and sophisticated, with looks that could make the finest matinee idol swoon (and did—Hammer's marketing pushed Lee as a sex symbol, and the public agreed in droves), Lee had already starred as the eponymous monster in *The Curse of Frankenstein*. This latest role was the one that would establish him as a star, however, and the one that would ensure he remained so.

After his ranking for more than six decades among Britain's top actors, it would be both disingenuous and somewhat insulting to claim that Sir Christopher Frank Carandini Lee CBE is *best* known to the world as Dracula. The role may have engaged him during the 1960s and early 1970s, when he established himself as Hammer's first and only choice for the part. But Lee personally ranked less than half of the movies he made in that guise as anything more than formulaic nonsense, and took justifiably far greater pride (and was far more appreciated by critics) in the roles he made his own in and around that sequence.

He was Scaramanga in *The Man with the Golden Gun*, one of the finest of the Roger Moore–era James Bond movies. He was Lord Summerisle in *The Wicker Man*, a 1973 movie that routinely comes close to the top of any poll of great British horror movies . . . and this one wasn't made by Hammer.

His other Hammer roles include Frankenstein, Sir Henry Baskerville, the Mummy, and a deeply sinister appearance as the leader of a Satanic coven in the studio's 1967 adaptation of Dennis Wheatley's *The Devil Rides Out*. He has portrayed M. R. James, the purveyor of so many wonderful ghost stories; and Jinnah, the founder of modern Pakistan. He is Flay in the BBC's gorgeous millennial production of Mervyn Peake's *Gormenghast*, and he executed Marie Antoinette in *La Révolution Française* (1989). He appeared as Count Dooku in the *Star Wars* prequels (oops, another count!) and Saruman in *The Lord of the Rings*, while he also ranks among Tim Burton's most regular stars . . . including an appearance (as fisherman Silas Clarney) in *Dark Shadows*. Dracula barely merits a footnote among such masterworks.

Born in London's Belgravia district on May 27, 1922, the son of a military man and a Swiss contessa, Lee divided his childhood between London and Switzerland following his parents' separation, and served with the Royal Air Force during World War II. Acting was a profession that had always interested him, but it was only following his return from the war that he considered pursuing it, and in 1947 he made his film debut in *Corridor of Mirrors*, a lightweight gothic romance directed by Terence Young.

Other roles followed, primarily small and often uncredited. His appearance as a spear bearer in Olivier's 1947 *Hamlet* is frequently mentioned as an early example of his rising star, when in fact his blink-and-you'll-miss-it cameo did not even make the movie's credits. Neither, although much has been made of the coincidence, can we divine anything from the appearance of Peter Cushing in the same movie. Yes, the pair would go on to costar in a wealth of films. But in *Hamlet*, they were not even close to appearing in the same scene.

It was Hammer who plucked Lee out of middling obscurity and established him as a star, and his appearance as the titular fiend in the first of the studio's vampire movies confirmed Lee as one of the three faces of British horror—the others, of course, were Cushing and Vincent Price. But while his work with the studio would consume much of the next two decades, Lee was forever cognizant with the dangers of being typecast as a fang-toothed freak in cape and red contacts. Hence his refusal to return to the Dracula role until 1965.

He has, in fact, appeared in almost as many Sherlock Holmes movies as Dracula ones, including roles in *The Hound of the Baskervilles* (Sir Henry, 1959), *Sherlock Holmes and the Deadly Necklace* (Holmes, 1962), *The Private Life of Sherlock Holmes* (brother Mycroft, 1970), *Incident at Victoria Falls* (Holmes, 1991) and *Sherlock Holmes and the Leading Lady* (Holmes, 1992). But other actors have already made Holmes their own, just as other actors have *tried* to make Dracula theirs. So disingenuity and insult be damned. Christopher Lee is Dracula, and he probably always will be.

Eschewing all of the blueprints established by the Lugosi Dracula movies, Hammer's *Dracula* returned to Bram Stoker, at least in terms of character and the rudiments of the plot. Jonathan Harker is the count's librarian; unbeknownst to his employer, however, he is something of a double agent, hired also by Van Helsing (Peter

Cushing) to destroy both the vampire and his wife (!). But he is turned before he completes the work, and when Van Helsing himself finally arrives at the castle, it is to discover Harker is as dangerous as Dracula, who in turn has become twice as dangerous as he seeks revenge for the death of his spouse.

And what a moment that was, the lovely Valerie Gaunt hissing and howling as she was staked through the heart, and then collapsing into a bag of haggish bones.

Dracula goes on the rampage. Lucy, Harker's fiancée, is taken. So is Mina, her brother Arthur's wife. But finally Van Helsing corners the count, and as the sun rises over their battleground, Dracula is vanquished.

So were the critics who more or less lined up to take turns at dismissing the movie as vile, sadistic nonsense; who could not be induced to find a single redeeming quality in a film that spent its entire running time sloshing about in buckets of blood; which was, according to the *Observer* newspaper, both "degraded and degrading." But audiences adored it; box office takings were phenomenal. And Hammer's name was set to become synonymous with horror.

With Dracula, too, although it would be a few years more before a follow-up was released. *The Revenge of Dracula* was already in the pipeline in 1958, when Christopher Lee announced he would not be returning to the role. But Hammer shrugged and marched on regardless, scrapping the Drac flick and reinventing another old Universal standard, the Mummy, instead. They lined up both the Hound of the Baskervilles and the Werewolf for adventures, then set sail across a sea of often inventive, and always entertaining, "lesser" vehicles. Hammer would not return to vamps until the dawn of the new decade.

THE BRIDES OF DRACULA (1960)

Dark forest, dread mountains, and dark, foreboding lakes ... Transylvania has never had better PR than it was granted by Hammer, and the thundering hooves and sea-sickening jolts of the carriage that crashes through the mist that opens *The Brides of Dracula* are so evocative that we can even forgive the Eastern European coach-man for sounding like an extra from *EastEnders*.

The Brides of Dracula circumvented Lee's reluctance to play the role by dismissing Dracula altogether from the plot and introducing in his stead Baron Meinster, an equally vicious and equally swoonworthy vampire (David Peel) who spends his nights (and days) in chains provided by his mother. No son of hers, she silently declaims, is going to despoil the family name by sucking the blood of the local villagers.

It does little to still the locals' fears. Habitually, they fall deathly silent whenever the magnificently haughty Baroness (Martita Hunt) marches into the local tavern to sample the wine and, as we join the action, to invite a stranded French student teacher to spend the night at her chateau. Where, unbeknownst to poor, trusting Marianne (Yvonne Monlaur), the Baroness intends to serve her up as a meal for her son, just the latest in the long line of mysterious disappearances that the villagers rarely even notice any longer. But this one is doomed to failure. Marianne meets the son, becomes utterly charmed, and instead of meekly offering him a midnight snack, agrees to free him from his bonds.

The Baron escapes, and Marianne continues on her journey in the company of a passing doctor whom she encountered on the road. It is Van Helsing (Cushing again), in the region to study "a strange sickness…the cult of the undead," and he becomes utterly enthralled by the girl's story of the wicked mother and the poor chained son. Especially after she informs him that the on-the-run Baron is now making regular trips to the school where she works. Where, of course, he is surrounded by delectable dishes. But Van Helsing is in no doubt whatsoever as to what the Baron's next meal should be.

A nice stake, of course. (Actually, it's the sails of a burning windmill, forming the shadow of a giant cross, but no matter.)

THE KISS OF THE VAMPIRE (1963)

Rasputin, the Gorgon, madmen, pirates—Hammer's remit was as broad as it was bloody. But always they returned to vampires, and every time, audiences leaped to applaud. *The Kiss of the Vampire* just gave them even more to cheer about than usual.

Once again, Lee was absent, and therefore, Dracula too—and one must applaud Hammer's insistence that only Lee was capable of playing the role. Any other franchise (as such continuing serials are now, unfortunately, known) would have simply mixed and matched whoever was available until you reach the point where we stand today, and every time Batman takes off his mask, he is wearing a different face beneath. No wonder the bad guys don't know who he is.

There again, it's not as if Dracula is the only mean, lean biting machine to be walking the Earth. *The Kiss of the Vampire* introduces us to Dr. Carl Ravna (played with slicked-back insouciance by Noel Willman), a vampire cult leader who is on the verge of hosting the annual bloodsucker's ball.

His home is Castle Dracula perfection, isolated and desolate, shrouded in night even when the sun shines, and the perfect place from which to spy upon any passing motorists who might run out of gas in the heart of his domain. The hapless Gerald and Marianne Harcourt eventually get a tow to the nearest hotel, but what a dowdy, derelict hole it is, its ruination rendered all the more foreboding when they discover that nobody has stayed there, or even visited the village, in a very, very long time.

An invitation to the castle to dine with Herr Doktor strikes the newlyweds as simple neighborliness. They are welcomed with warmth and dignity, and introduced to the Doctor's adult children. They are wined and dined. It all seems so civilized. And it actually takes a while before they learn the error of their ways. But learn it they do, as the Doctor and his increasingly sinister-seeming brood inveigle their way into the couple's trust, and then spring their evil trap.

Fortunately for them, and especially for Marianne, the local vampire killer, Professor Zimmer, is on hand to effect a rescue. Which he does by securely binding the castle with garlic to ensure no vampire can escape, and then summoning up a horde of fabulously flapping, swooping, biting bats from Hell to destroy them. And yes, you did read that correctly.

Two points worth making before you smirk, however (three if you include *Rocky Horror*'s obvious debt). First, Roman Polanski was surely homaging *The Kiss of the Vampire* when he echoed the masked ball in *The Fearless Vampire Killers*. And second, Alfred Hitchcock had not yet started work on *The Birds* when *The Kiss of the Vampire* unleashed its utterly believable, flapping, swooping, biting flock of bats. But he soon would.

DRACULA: PRINCE OF DARKNESS (1966)

It's hard to decide what to like best about *Dracula: Prince of Darkness*. Was it the return of Christopher Lee, for the first time since the original Hammer *Dracula*? Was it director Terence Fisher likewise returning to the scene of some of his greatest crimes? Was it the effervescent beauty of Barbara Shelley? Or was it all of these things and more, gathered together beneath a truly unforgettable title, while the count seeks only to put the bite on a young couple named Charles and Diana?

One would never say of a Hammer film that "no expense was spared." While never appearing cheap, still Hammer relished its status as purveyor of a superior breed of B-movie, and although the studio was certainly responsible for its fair share of cinematic innovation (*The Curse of Frankenstein* was the first-ever British horror movie to be shot in color), it was also a dab hand at cutting corners.

So sharp eyes and cynical dispositions can probably sit and pick fault with all of *Prince of Darkness*'s special effects. But you need to be a true killjoy to even begin to doubt the veracity of Dracula's revival scene, as a heap of ashes shift and stir first into the form of a skeleton, which becomes a vaguely humanoid puddle of guts, and finally emerges as a naked man, sleeping like a babe in his sarcophagus. And audiences gasped, not because they had never before seen a naked man (and you couldn't see much, to be truthful), but because they had never before seen a vampire who did not return to life in full cape and costuming.

A few caveats. Although this is unquestionably Lee's movie, the actor scarcely distinguishes himself in the role, his vocal performance being so limited that Howard Maxford, author of the definitive Hammer biography (*Hammer House of Horror: Behind the Screams*—Overlook Press, 1996) refers to him as "little more than a hissing bogeyman."

Likewise, the plot, the resolution, and even the appearance of yet another elderly vampire hunter (Andrew Keir as Father Sandor) are all such standard devices that the movie's thrills unquestionably walk hand in hand with déjà vu. But that's not a bad thing, and besides, what is the point of having a winning formula if you're just going to change it around all the time? Because right now, ten years after first dipping a toe into the horror waters, Hammer was winning all the time.

DRACULA HAS RISEN FROM THE GRAVE (1968)

Rasputin the Mad Monk, with Christopher Lee at his loquacious best; *The Witches*; *Plague of the Zombies*; *The Reptile*; *One Million Years B.C.*; *Frankenstein Created Woman*; *The Viking Queen*; *The Lost Continent*; *The Devil Rides Out*; and the long-awaited conclusion to the Quatermass trilogy, *Quatermass and the Pit*—all these and more slithered out of Hammer's Bray Studios complex during 1966–1968.

And so did *Dracula Has Risen from the Grave*, Christopher Lee scrambling out of the icy resting place into which he was plunged at the conclusion of the last movie, to generally rip, roar, and rend his way through a succession of luckless passersby.

It is not, by past standards, that great a film; rather, it is something of a potboiler, distinguished more by individual scenes and setups than by any internal logic. But we smile as Hammer repays Polanski for his Jewish vampire joke by having Lee jerk a stake out of his own heart with an admonition that borders on "Tut tut, must do better," and we witness one of the series' great reveals, as a young girl's corpse is discovered inside a giant bell.

We also see Lee at his best, not through the script or direction, but in his own approach to the role. No matter how powerful Dracula was, Lee brought a certain vulnerability to the character, a certain sadness. "It's not in the dialogue itself," Lee explained to *The Monster Times* in 1972. "It's …expressed in an occasional way of saying something. The sadness may not have come to me in the course of doing the first Hammer *Dracula*. Perhaps it was something that struck me later. I don't exactly recall."

Dracula's demise, too, is beautifully staged, impaled upon a giant golden cross—a scene that author Chrissie Bentley had in mind when she employed a similar device at the conclusion of her erotic vamp romp *Taste the Blood of Dracula*. Which just happens to be the title of the next movie in the Hammer sequence.

TASTE THE BLOOD OF DRACULA (1970) / SCARS OF DRACULA (1970)

By the turn of the decade, Christopher Lee was making no secret of the fact that he was tiring of the Dracula role, even going so far as to publicly criticize both this latest movie and its success. "I have got past understanding any of this," he sighed at the time, and for once the critics agreed with him. They hated it as much as ever; now Lee seemed to be joining them.

As is always the case when new life is breathed into an old body, the 1960s had seen a number of movie makers attempt to ape the Hammer success story, and it would be remiss not to at least fleetingly mention a handful of the films that hit the movie theaters with one eye definitely focused upon the British studio's golden goose.

The infamous output of director William Beaudine—a sequence of calumnies that stretched back to 1953's *Bela Lugosi Meets a Brooklyn Gorilla* and forward to *Billy the Kid vs. Dracula* a decade later—does not concern us. The movies were certainly appalling, but they were also intended, at least nominally, to be comedies, and the latter, the world's first Transylvanian Western, actually tries hard to convince us it was a good idea. It fails, but it tries, and at least it's superior to yet another Beaudine bruiser, *Jesse James Meets Frankenstein's Daughter*.

But what can we make of *A Taste of Blood* (1967), a two-hour Herschell G. Lewis marathon in which a businessman inadvertently drinks from a bottle of Dracula's blood and is transformed into a vampire? Two hours. Bowel surgery has been known to take less time than that. Or 1969's *Blood of Dracula's Castle*, director Al

Adamson's vision of Dracula's life in modern America? Around such nasties, entire genres can be crippled, and the vampire movie of the age was certainly feeling the first pangs of atrophy.

None of which would prevent Christopher Lee from reprising the role as the cameras rolled on *Taste the Blood of Dracula*, a movie that transports the count to Victorian England to cavort amid the twisted moralities of that era.

Three pleasure-seeking gentlemen, enacting their own vision of the legendary Hellfire Club, fall under the influence of the aristocratic Lord Courtley, who sets them a fascinating task: to procure for him a phial of the dried blood of Dracula.

This they do, and spellbound, we watch as Courtley revives his master, only to die in the process. Which is the cue for Dracula to set about some good old-fashioned vengeance seeking, a rampage that is surely his most sexually unambiguous yet. Young women, of whom there are plenty, all but throw themselves at the handsome count, regardless of the fatal sucking they are destined to receive, while scenes in an East London bordello could have been swept from an especially seedy retelling of the Jack the Ripper saga.

This fresh permissiveness dances, too, through the second of that year's Dracula movies, *Scars of Dracula*, an offering that can reasonably claim to be the most bloodthirsty of all the Count's celluloid adventures. Scarcely a scene goes by without something nasty either happening or being considered, but two stick in the mind: Dracula torturing Doctor Who (the Second Doctor, Patrick Troughton) with a whip and a red-hot poker, and the gore-spattered death of the lovely Anouska Hempel, the vampire Tania. Bad enough that she should be stabbed in the stomach by the rampaging count. Even worse that he should then drink the blood that gushes from the wound. And yes, the symbolism was apparent to all.

Audience numbers for these movies were among the lowest Hammer had ever experienced for a new release, particularly for one of their most vaunted headline attractions. Rather than change course, however, the studio opted instead to change the focus. 1970–1971 brought the arrival of the aforementioned sagas of Carmilla and of Elisabeth Bathory, half a dozen movies that pursued the concept of lesbian vampires toward heights—and depths—that many contemporary critics regarded as bordering upon the pornographic, featuring a vampire who probably remains the most sexually alluring creature her species has ever bred.

THE VAMPIRE LOVERS (1970)

Born Kasha Kotuzova in Poland on November 21, 1937, and raised in East Berlin following her family's release from a Nazi concentration camp in 1945, actress Ingrid Pitt is to many people the female face of Hammer Horror, and that despite appearing in a mere pair of the studio's classic movies.

The roles she played, however, and the vivacity that she brought to them has ensured that hers is usually the first name anybody remembers when recalling the bevy of beauties whom casting filed through the Hammer machine throughout the 1960s and early 1970s—a roll call that includes the likes of singer Dana Gillespie, '80s soap stars Stephanie Beacham and Kate O'Mara, Bond girl Ursula Andress, Raquel Welch, Nastassja Kinski, and *AbFab*'s Joanna Lumley.

A member of the Bertolt Brecht Berliner Ensemble in her teens, Pitt escaped to the West by swimming across the River Spee, assisted by her husband-to-be, an American soldier. She joined him in the US but returned to Europe after the marriage ended (she retained her married name, Pitt) and from 1964, became a familiar face in a succession of low-budget Spanish movies. That period ended when, in 1968, she was cast as the double agent Heidi in *Where Eagles Dare*, and the following year, a meeting with Hammer's James Carreras saw her offered the role of Carmilla in the upcoming *The Vampire Lovers*.

She relished the role, and the camera relished her. Costarring alongside the wide-eyed beauty of Madeleine Smith (one of the miniskirted dollies in *Taste the Blood of Dracula*), with whom she performed one of the most convincing lesbian love scenes of the era, Pitt *became* Carmilla. Indeed, had the wheels not already fallen off Hammer's vampire bus, as audiences grew sparse and the critics' complaints became more justified, there is little doubt that Pitt's career in that role would have far exceeded the mere two movies it stretched to—although behind the scenes, there were other reasons.

Arguing with producers Harry Fine and Michael Style, Pitt was passed over for the same role in the sequel *Lust for a Vampire* (Yutte Stensgaard replaced her). Compensation arrived, however, with her casting as the Countess Elisabeth Bathory in *Countess Dracula* (1971), a movie that was even bloodier, and revealed even more naked flesh, than *The Vampire Lovers*. But Pitt's association with Hammer was at an end.

She continued to thrill. She is a vivid presence in *The House That Dripped Blood* (1971) and appeared alongside Christopher Lee in 1973's *The Wicker Man*; she moved into television and also ignited a career as a successful novelist. There was even a rapprochement with the Hammer name, when she was cast in the revived company's 2007 movie *Beyond the Rave* (sadly, her appearance was cut from the final film).

Pitt passed away on November 23, 2010.

DRACULA A.D. 1972 (1972)

The early 1970s' apparent obsession with ever more erotic exhibitionism was not wholly Hammer's problem, nor uniquely their undoing. Cinema in general was experiencing a serious sea change at the time, as established studios, directors, and actors struggled to come to grips with the tide of "anything goes" permissiveness that had burbled from the underground at the end of the 1960s—a wave that was only broadened by society's apparent acceptance of undiluted pornography in the form of 1972's *Deep Throat*.

The first true porn movie to breach the American mainstream, and the catalyst for the tsunami of similarly themed films that followed it into the main street multiplex, *Deep Throat* may still have been regarded as indecent in the eyes of the law and society at large. But its massive success, and the fact that it drew approving comments from even the highest echelons of the entertainment industry, opened a door that only that most nebulous of regulators, "common decency," prevented the rest of the film industry from bundling through.

Now the race was on for "mainstream" cinema to replicate the sexual thrill of *Deep Throat, Behind the Green Door*, and so many others without actually resorting to filming the sexual act itself. At the same time as shoehorning such sequences into a movie that people might want to watch for reasons other than undiluted voyeurism.

A few succeeded, but far more failed, and in the UK, where the British Board of Film Censors remained implacably opposed to even the loosening standards of their American cousins, attempts to shoot a mainstream sex film inevitably looked toward the comedy genre. *Percy* was the tale of the world's first penis transplant—and the penis's subsequent quest to reacquaint itself with every woman its previous owner had slept with; the *Confessions* series demonstrated the perks of the job that await driving instructors and window cleaners; and so forth.

Transplanting what those films reduced to comic ribaldry into movies where such sniggering had no place was a considerably more difficult task, and it was one that Hammer, sadly, was not capable of fulfilling. Unless, of course, you happen to love *Dracula A.D. 1972*, a production that revels in such base camp that you could launch a mountaineering expedition from within.

Dracula is reborn in modern-day London, courtesy of a band of teenaged kick seekers led by the appallingly named Johnny Alucard. He finds himself in Chelsea, the nexus (albeit a few years earlier) of Swinging London, and had he only ventured out of the derelict church in which he was revived, the count would doubtless have been both astonished and appalled by the amount of flesh that was on everyday display. It was the heyday, of course, of the miniskirt, and with Hammer's casting department having stuffed the movie with girls who looked especially good in such costuming, clearly the scene was set for some gloriously garish action.

Sadly, and still capable of spoiling the movie for the majority of viewers, whoever wrote the script had even less of an ear for teenaged slang than the wardrobe department had an eye for fashion. The coffee-bar scenes would have felt embarrassingly stilted in the late 1950s, when people (at least in movies) really did talk like this, and one almost feels sorry for Peter Cushing, returning as Van Helsing for the first time since *The Brides of Dracula*. But not for Christopher Lee, who really, really should have known better.

THE SATANIC RITES OF DRACULA (1973)

Still, the pair reunited for one final battle, as *The Satanic Rites of Dracula* (1973) dredged up another of the series' most evocative titles (it was certainly better than the original choice, *Dracula Is Dead and Well and Living in London*), and then deployed it on a script that could as easily have doubled as an apocalyptic ecodrama. Van Helsing is the determined hero who emotes his way into saving the world; Dracula is a mad American billionaire whose unwitting stooge, an otherwise brilliant scientist, has perfected a bacterium that can destroy it.

Joanna Lumley, later to find massive fame courtesy of *The New Avengers* and *Absolutely Fabulous*, plays Van Helsing's dolly-bird granddaughter, Jessica (a role first broached in the previous movie by Stephanie Beecham), and the count himself lives in a gadget-packed dwelling straight out of James Bond. Oh, and there's a biker gang looking ever so menacing in their sheepskin jackets.

Fabulous opening credits unfold with Dracula's silhouette expanding menacingly over a tourist-board trip around the sights of London, before we journey to a secluded mansion where the human sacrifice being prepared downstairs is brilliantly upstaged by the escape of the battered soul being held prisoner by the bikers on an upper story. None of this appears to make much sense, but all will be revealed as the movie unfolds, and a byzantine plot begins to take shape around the government minister, wealthy landowner, and military top brass who are members of the coven, and the secret agents who suddenly realize they're investigating their boss.

A political thriller, then, with nothing more sinister taking place than a bunch of bored weirdoes using Satanism as a shield for orgies and kinky kicks. Until Van Helsing, an "authority in the occult," is called in, just as the slaughtered girl arises from the altar, just as the reborn Dracula takes his first victim, just as Van Helsing unearths the existence of the disease.

The occasional scene packs all the old thrills. The sacrifice is very well done, and we get a terrific moment in the crypt, with Jessica assaulted by a veritable bevy of vamped-up victims. There's also a lovely (if possibly unintentional) homage to Dreyer's *Vampyr* when the first of Dracula's kills, a civil-service clerk named Jane (Valerie Van Ost), turns slowly to echo Sybille Schmitz's most feral grin at the outset of the terrified Jessica's ordeal.

The Satanic Rites of Dracula is often regarded as the last of Hammer's Transylvanian twists, and maybe it should have been. No longer the lair of the creature feature, Hammer was striking out in search of new genres to merge with its established properties. So when high-stakes espionage didn't pan out, and the following year's *Captain Kronos: Vampire Hunter* failed to launch a new action hero onto the world, so another bag of plasma was attached to the drip feed, to spill out into a movie that you really only need watch for the sake of saying you've seen every vampire film the studio ever made. And even then, you shouldn't say it too loudly. It is called *The Legend of the Seven Golden Vampires*, and grown men tremble at its very mention.

THE LEGEND OF THE SEVEN GOLDEN VAMPIRES (1974)

The studio was nearing the end of its lifespan, the victim not only of its own success but of its inability to resist recycling the successes of the past. Like those desperate trailers for movies that try to interest you in one movie because it is from "the makers/producers/caterers of" another, Hammer had started to believe its own publicity, while forgetting that a lot of that publicity was self-generated.

There were bigger and better horror films being made and released now; 1972 brought Jim O'Connolly's protoslasher epic *The Tower of Evil* (a.k.a. *Horror on Snape Island*); 1973 delivered *The Wicker Man*, and then eclipsed all that had gone before with *The Ex-*

orcist. Compared with these, the very name Hammer had become a byword for schlocky late-night television movies. And if that was the fate of the classics, shot when the studio was sparking with invention, imagine what the later flicks were like.

The Legend of the Seven Golden Vampires, as its title attempted to suggest, was set in the Far East (and shot in Hong Kong), Van Helsing hot on the trail of the last survivors of a vampire cult led, of course, by Dracula (played, in Lee's understandable absence, by John Forbes-Robertson). Through the streets of Edwardian Chungking they go, but no normal vampire chase is this. For these vamps know kung fu!

It is a sad affair. Few of the local actors recruited to the movie spoke English, so the film was shot in silence and then dubbed. The entire musical soundtrack needed to be rewritten at the last minute when the original Hong Kong–sourced tapes turned out to be even worse than the movie they were intended to accompany. And the story, frankly, is silly.

Barely distributed, scarcely even noticed, the movie sank like a stone. Unless they were lucky (?) enough to live in the Far East itself, where the movie apparently enjoyed some success, even Hammer connoisseurs had to work hard to see it—and work even harder to remain in their seats while it played. It was a sad, sad ending to both Peter Cushing's career as Van Helsing and to Hammer's own output. The studio had already returned to its prehorror standard of making movie versions of top television hits, sitcoms for the most part, but by 1976, even they had dried up.

The Hammer had fallen.

THE CARPATHIAN EAGLE (1980)

There was a rebirth of sorts in the early 1980s, when Hammer Films undertook two series of hour-long horror stories for British television, *The Hammer House of Horror* and *The Hammer House of Mystery and Suspense*, with the first at least packing no less than thirteen hours' worth of thrills and spills.

Mostly set in the same unspoiled English countryside that had not only become redolent of Hammer's classic era but still permeates the world of British TV detectives and murder mysteries, where every house is timbered and every lane is leafy, *The Hammer House of Horror* embraced all of the studio's old obsessions. Witches (heralded by Patricia Quinn in one of her finest TV roles), demons, and werewolves all went roaming through the gloaming, and when the series peaked, it did so with its wildest installment yet. *Carpathian Eagle* follows police detective Cliff (Anthony Valentine) as he sets out on the trail of a serial killer whose modus operandi leaves little room for copycats. The victim's heart has been carved out with a knife.

This is baffling enough to begin with, but grows even more bizarre after the cop catches the end of a radio spot discussing a new book about a three-hundred-year old countess who, with Bathoryesque brutality, dispatched her victims in precisely the same fashion.

Meeting with the author (Suzanne Danielle), Cliff is introduced to the countess's last surviving relative, a kindly old lady who gladly sums up the story: How the countess committed adultery while her husband was away at the wars; how he discovered her sin and cruelly tortured her for weeks on end—until that one dark night when her pet eagle tore out the sadistic count's heart. And from then on, the countess ruled the land, taking a succession of handsome young lovers and dispatching each of them in a similar manner.

The police investigation continues. So do the killings. And while we, the viewers, have already met the murderess, a beautiful brunette with a deep, exotic accent, we are yet to discover precisely who she is. But we will.

As an updating of the legends that fired *Countess Dracula* a decade before, fed through with a cocktail bar's worth of twists, the discovery that the old woman is not the *very* last member of the family is only the first of the scheduled shocks. There is also a nephew, an escapee from Communist Europe, who happens to work as a female impersonator. A beautiful brunette with a deep, exotic accent.

Case closed? You'd rather think so, wouldn't you?...

BEYOND THE RAVE (2007)

Periodically over the next quarter of a century, rumors would circulate of the Hammer name returning to the big screen. It was 2007, however, before there was true cause for celebration, when MySpace hosted the first all-new Hammer production in almost thirty years, the four-part, eighty-minute *Beyond the Rave.*

"All they wanted," warn the posters, "was a night to remember." Ed (Jamie Dornan) is a military man, a soldier enjoying his final night at home before being shipped out to Iraq the following day. He and his friend Necro decide to spend their time searching for Ed's girlfriend, Jen, last seen heading off to a rave in a forest.

They find her, and discover also that the rave is simply a blind, organized by a vampire cult led by the sinister Melech, and designed to provide the revelers with an ample supply of blood before they set off on what they describe as a long sea journey. Which seems very old-fashioned of them, but hey! Vampires *like* old-fashioned.

It's not a bad movie, either. Sadie Frost, Lucy in Coppola's *Bram Stoker's Dracula*, appears as one of the vampires, Fallen Angel; and Ingrid Pitt, aforementioned heroine of classic Hammer fare, almost makes an appearance as the mother of a drug dealer ... "almost" because her scene was cut for the final version, although her name remains in the credits. In fact the only real drawback is that the four parts on MySpace represented just two-thirds of the full feature, with the final two episodes available only on a DVD that itself was a strictly limited edition.

Still Hammer was back, and they were about to become big again, too.

LET THE RIGHT ONE IN (2008) / LET ME IN (2010)

A lot of movies can be (and have been) described as one of the greatest vampire flicks of all time. But generally there's a caveat of one kind or another. Not this time though. This time, the honor is unequivocal. *Let the Right One In* (2008) is the best vampire movie ever made.

In terms of mood, storytelling, atmosphere, and performance, it is certainly up there, just as the original novel ranks among the best vampire stories ever told. In terms of capturing the true bittersweet symphony of being, or loving, a vampire, however, it streaks ahead. No other movie captures the balance of power and pathos so effectively as this.

Female vampires, as we have already seen (and will see again in chapter 10), are no rarity in either the literature or its celluloid spin-offs. Juvenile female vampires, however, are less common. And juvenile female vampires who are not simply bit players alongside a more mature role model (Kirsten Dunst as Claudia in *Interview with the Vampire* springs to mind) are scarcer than corpuscles in a corpse. *Let the Right One In* redresses the balance.

In its original book form, *Låt den Rätte Komma In* was the 2004 literary debut by John Ajvide Lindqvist, now established as one of his native Sweden's greatest horror writers (if you like zombies, you will love *Hanteringen av Odöda* [*Handling the Undead*], his 2005 follow-up).

It is the tale of Oskar (played onscreen by Kåre Hedebrant), a twelve-year-old boy who is the subject of constant bullying at school, and who retreats into a private world of daydreamed vengeance and vendetta. In fact, he is rehearsing for one such assault, hacking at a tree with a knife, when he is disturbed by a stranger, a girl named Eli (Lina Leandersson) who has just moved into the apartment next to the one Oskar shares with his mother in a grim working-class corner of Stockholm's Blackeberg suburb.

So far, so heartwarming. Eli will teach Oskar not to be afraid, to fight back—a role that neither his clinging mother nor his estranged father seems capable of adopting. There is just one slight drawback. Eli is a vampire, turned two centuries before, and living, since then, in the body of a child who gets by through the kindness of a succession of older men attracted by her helplessness and vulnerability. Or, as *Elle*'s review put it, "In a performance devoid of sentimentality she perfectly captures the awful solitude of a creature who exists outside time."

Her latest consort is Håkan, a thoroughly disreputable middle-aged man who hunts the living and drains their blood into a bucket, to take home to Eli in the hope that tonight will be the night when she will allow him to live out his fantasies with her. But she never has, and she never will, probably because the expeditions that the camera accompanies him on all end in abject failure: the first when he is disturbed by a woman walking her dog, the second when he is caught in the act.

He takes the only way out, one that he has already prepared for. He pours acid over his own head in the hope of both dying and rendering his corpse unrecognizable. He will prove successful too. But not immediately. Nor later, after Eli drains him. The novel (but not the movie) has a lot more in store for poor, pathetic Håkan, and suddenly a suburb that was on edge because of one string of disappearances, and the rumor of a single vampire, is faced with a string of vicious murders and the knowledge that there is now another.

The original Swedish-language version of the movie, from 2008, is the classic—even the imposition of some positively unwatchable English subtitles to the original US DVD release (subsequently replaced by the original theatrical text) could not disturb the tranquil beauty of the movie, nor deplete the horror, both visual and implied.

Inevitably, then, any attempt to remake it for an English-speaking audience was going to suffer by comparison. But that is the only manner in which Hammer's *Let Me In* is found wanting. Transplanted from Stockholm to New Mexico, and with Oskar and Eli now named Owen and Abby, *Let Me In* is surprisingly faithful to the book, and somehow contrives to be even more violent than its predecessor.

The scene in which Virginia, one of Eli/Abby's victims, rids herself of the vampire curse by exposing herself to sunlight in the hospital, for example, results in just one charred corpse in the Swedish movie. Hammer demanded two, and so an attending nurse is barbecued alongside her bedridden patient.

The love story that lies beneath both movies, meanwhile, echoes nothing so much as that which propels the 1971 romance *Melody*, a movie that could not be any further from either the vampire or horror genres if it tried. And just as viewers of that delightful film have spent the intervening decades wondering what became of Daniel and Melody, so everybody from the first reviewers on had their own suspicions about why Eli was so taken by Oskar—particularly when the story ends with the pair of them leaving town on a train, Oskar in his seat and Eli, because it is daylight, in a box.

Could she, perhaps, have been grooming him all along, unspooling another layer of abuse into a movie that really can leave a bad taste in the mouth of anyone who watches it from that particular perspective? Apparently not. Stung by accusations that he claims never to have even considered when he wrote the story, Lindqvist followed up with the short story "Låt de Gamla Drömmarna Dö" ("Let the Old Dreams Die"), tracing the subsequent adventures of the pair. It is a conclusion that both deserve.

Léone (Sybille Schmitz) in the thrall of Carl Theodor Dreyer's *Vampyr* (1932). (General Foreign Sales Corp./Photofest)

10

THE LADY IS A VAMP:
THE GIRLS GO FOR THE JUGULAR

The Brides of Dracula are almost as old a concept as that of Dracula himself. They appear in Bram Stoker's original story, the weird sisters who flirt and float through the castle, feasting upon whomever they can snare with their beautifully manicured nails, and they drift silently through most of the subsequent movie adaptations and revisions.

Nevertheless, they have remained bit players, which is something of a disappointment. Partly because their story, for sure, would be a fascinating one. But also because without at least one of the brides, it's unlikely we would ever have experienced Universal's second contribution to the vampire canon, *Dracula's Daughter.*

Female vampires are, in a lot of ways, subjective creatures. For many years, until as late as the the 1930s, *vampire* was very much a double-barreled word, as likely to be used to describe a Transylvanian bloodsucker as it was a certain type of woman, whose feminine wiles and guiles were employed to drain their victims not of blood but of money (or in the case of Bill Compton's vamp of a vamp maker Lorena Krasiki, both at once). Indeed, there is a great line in *Dracula's Daughter*, as the hunter sets out with stake and hammer and tells his butler he is vampire hunting.

"I thought you usually went after them with a checkbook," replies his doughty servant.

Dracula's Daughter, then, was America's introduction to the cinematic stealth of the lady vamp. Europe, however, met her a few years earlier.

VAMPYR (1932)

At the same time as Bela Lugosi's *Dracula* was shocking audiences across the English-speaking world, Danish director Carl Theodor Dreyer was at work on *Vampyr*, eschewing Stoker for Le Fanu, and then deleting *Carmilla*'s subtext of a beautiful vampiress feeding on the lifeblood of young girls in favor of the aged crone Marguerite Chopin (Henriette Gérard), for whom an intake of blood is essential if she is to revert to the beauty of her youth.

In truth, *Vampyr* is a difficult slog, more of an exercise in exploring a myth than exploiting a story, and neither possessing nor providing much in the way of shocks. At least until the scene in the bedroom, where Léone (Sybille Schmitz), Chopin's latest victim, turns her most feral grin toward her sister, poor Giselle. That moment is worth the entire cost of admission.

One of the undisputed beauties of German film, Schmitz was still a comparative unknown to cinema audiences when she was recruited to *Vampyr*. Already into her thirties, she learned her trade in the theater during the last years of the Weimar Republic (her first engagement was at Max Reinhardt's Deutsches Theater in Berlin in 1927), and would not come to true acclaim until later in the 1930s, by which time German cinema was firmly in the thrall of Hitler's Third Reich.

Her actual work was apolitical, and the stream of movies she made during the ensuing decade included several that would, had they been shot under any other regime, be regarded as classics today: *Abschiedswalzer* (*Parting Waltz*) (1934), in which Schmitz appears as George Sand, the lover of the composer Frédéric Chopin; *Skandal um Gloria* (1935), a sharp revision of Oscar Wilde's *An Ideal Husband*; and *Fährmann Maria* (*Ferryboat Woman Maria*) (1936), a magnificent supernatural blockbuster filled with mysterious horsemen, swirling mists, looming forests, and ominous ferrymen.

Here Schmitz plays Maria, turning in a performance that movie historian David Stewart Hull terms "one of her most Garboesque . . . the embodiment of womanly virtue and steadfast faith," but which Goebbels, overseeing the Nazi's movie industry, loathed so much that the film was all but suppressed in Germany. (Director

Frank Wysbar later remade it as *Strangler of the Swamp*, following his postwar emigration to the US.)

Schmitz continued working. She is vivacious in 1938's *Der Tanz auf dem Vulkan* (*Dance on the Volcano*); outstanding in *Wetterleuchten um Barbara* (*Summer Lightning on Barbara*), a 1940 look back at the Nazi annexation of Austria; and only a poor script truly derails her role as Empress Maria Theresa in *Trenck, der Pandur* (1940). But perhaps her greatest post-*Vampyr* role is one that also illustrates for the modern reader just how ruthlessly all evidence of a Nazi-run German film industry was expunged in the years following the war. In 1943, Schmitz was cast as Sigrid, a beautiful and enigmatic woman who emerges as one of the heroines of the sinking of the *Titanic*, in director Herbert Selpin's movie of the same name.

Titanic had already arrived in the cinemas battered and bruised. The director was murdered by the Gestapo while filming was still underway, and the censors hacked the movie to pieces once it was completed. Whereas the postwar era should have seen it restored and proclaimed a masterpiece, however, it then suffered the most ignominious fate of all. Buried away in the Allied archives, it was not seen again until its spectacular recreation of the doomed ocean liner's last moments were spliced into the 1958 British movie *A Night to Remember*, without a word of acknowledgment or apology.

Unlike so many of her contemporaries, Schmitz survived the war and the ensuing occupations, and might have hoped for her career to resume once the German film industry was back on its feet. Instead, her labors during the dark years of recent memory were not to be forgiven, and like director Leni Riefenstahl (and many others), Schmitz was essentially blackballed at a time when, if *Titanic* is any measure, she was at the height of her talents.

Neither would she be rehabilitated. Her fortieth birthday was looming, and Schmitz was largely unemployable, just a few small roles that kept her ticking over. She spiraled into decline, drugs and alcohol igniting a depression that led to several suicide attempts and, finally, a stint in psychiatric care. The treatment was unsuccessful; released into the care of a physician, Ursula Moritz, Schmitz died from an overdose of sleeping pills in April 1955. It later came to light that Moritz was both selling and administering drugs to the actress throughout the entire time she was in her charge.

Schmitz's vampire could be described as a foreshadowing of this tragic life. She is not a seductress; she does not adhere to any of the term's other meanings. She is sick, she is weak, she is scared. She does not seek a cure for her condition; she merely laments her conviction that her death is at hand, and with it an eternity of damnation. This early into the vampire's cinematic lifespan, Schmitz brought us what remains perhaps the most heartrending portrayal of the true meaning of the curse.

DRACULA'S DAUGHTER (1936)

It took Universal five years to follow up the runaway success of *Dracula*—five years during which the legend of the count hung in a limbo of sorts, and American cinema audiences grew gray with worry over whether they'd ever see their favorite vamp again.

They would, but he would not, initially, be recognizable. Lugosi was out of the picture, and so was Dracula himself. Instead, the story switched to the Countess Marya Zaleska (Gloria Holden), the titular daughter and a most unwilling perpetrator of the bloodline. Indeed, with the death of her father at the end of the previous movie, her greatest hope is that she will now be free of the family curse—free to become a human being.

It doesn't happen. Neither can anything else help; she turns to psychiatry, and when that doesn't work, she resorts to kidnapping, dragging her doctor Jeffrey Garth (Otto Kruger) back to Transylvania with her, in the belief that even if she cannot have humanity, she can at least find love. Little does she realize that she has already been ensnared in someone else's fantasies: a manservant, Sandor, who is sparked to such peaks of jealousy that he shoots the countess with an arrow and kills her.

It was an intriguing treatment, all the more so since it claimed to be based on a Bram Stoker short story, "Dracula's Guest"—whose own plot appears utterly absent from the movie. But Holden's performance is wonderful: gracious, mesmeric, and absolutely spellbinding every moment she spends on the screen. *Dracula's*

Daughter would not be the smash hit that Universal was hoping for when it was made. But in many ways, it is superior to its predecessor. Which establishes it as a very rare sequel indeed.

BLACK SUNDAY (LA MASCHERA DEL DEMONIO / THE MASK OF SATAN) (1960)

La Maschera del Demonio (*The Mask of Satan*)—or, as it is more commonly known in English, *Black Sunday*—is one of the masterpieces of Italian cinema, dating from that glorious period during which the country's cinematic output was almost guaranteed to keep the average ketchup maker in business for years.

Black Sunday is no exception. It opens with a witch, Asa Vajda (the stunning Barbara Steele), being condemned to death by her own brother: sentenced to be burned alive having first had a metal mask nailed to her face.

She perishes in the flames . . . which probably doesn't explain how her perfectly preserved corpse now awaits rediscovery two centuries on, the mask still in place beneath the glass frontal of her burial place. Yes, glass. Upon which a passing doctor will cut his hand (having broken it while swiping at a low-flying bat), allowing a few drops of blood to fall upon Asa's corpse. She returns to life and, in so doing, is able to reanimate the lover who perished with her, Javuto. And together, transformed into ruthless, vengeful vampires, a-bloodletting they will go.

It sounds so hokey, doesn't it? But *Black Sunday* was regarded as being so gruesomely, gratuitously violent that it was banned from distribution in the UK until 1968 (and unseen in its uncut form until 1992), while US prints were butchered almost as badly as some of Asa's victims before it could be screened.

None of this halted the growth of its legend. Intending to demolish the movie as a crock of sensationalist nonsense, the *New York Times* condemned Steele as "a blank-eyed manikin with an earthbound figure and a voice from outer space." But that was as much a component of her appeal, and her success, as any other—the one-sheet poster that accompanied the movie on its US release demanded that cinemagoers "stare into these eyes," and they too portrayed Asa as otherworldly, vivacious, and vacantly wide eyed.

More than that, Asa stands as the most successful vampiric reinvention of the entire post-Universal, pre-Hammer's golden age (the first *Dracula* movie was less than two years old at the time), and the first truly successful distillation of feminine beauty and sensuality as the epitome of evil.

It would prove startlingly influential, too. Francis Ford Coppola's take on *Dracula* thirty years later included several homages to *Black Sunday*, while Tim Burton, interviewed in a documentary biography of director Mario Bava, explained, "One of the movies that remain with me probably stronger than anything is *Black Sunday.*...The vibe and the feeling is what it's about ... a mixture of eroticism, of sex, of horror and starkness of image, and to me that is more real than what most people would consider realism in films."

BLOOD AND ROSES (*ET MOURIR DE PLAISIR*) (1960)

Roger Vadim's *Blood and Roses* is the story of jealousy and the lengths to which it will drive its victims, wrapped around imagery and chills lifted from Le Fanu's *Carmilla*—Vadim's heroine, Carmilla de Karnstein (his wife, Annette), takes her name from her, and we discover very early on that the family has its own vampire tradition, tucked away in a family cemetery that the locals have feared for centuries.

We learn, too, that Carmilla has long been fascinated by the legend of an eighteenth-century ancestor named Millarca (spot the anagram), who died in her lover Ludwig's arms, but whose vampiric spirit sustained itself by feeding on the women with whom Ludwig became involved in years to come. Carmilla walks to the woman's portrait. "Don't you think she looks like me?"

Carmilla's calm recitation of the legend to her cousin Leopoldo (Mel Ferrer)'s fiancée, Georgia (Elsa Martinelli), disguises her hatred for the girl; she absents herself from the engagement party by getting drunk and staging one of her own, on her own. He is enraged, she is furious, and Millarca's voiceover, so seductive and sensual, whispers of her growing possession of Carmilla. The next time we see Carmilla, she is statuesque in the last outfit her ancestor ever wore in life, the wedding dress in which she died. And when a series of mysterious explosions rip through the cemetery during the party's firework display, Carmilla is drawn to the vampire's crypt.

"The stone is cold, but underneath, I am warm. Touch the stone, Carmilla ... touch the stone."

Consumed by the spirit of her forebear, Carmilla's stalking of the servant girl Lisa plays out with all the delicacy of a game of kiss chase until the girl realizes the chase is at an end and the kiss is the last thing she will ever feel. But even her death only moistens the palate, as the vampire sets about hunting the biggest game of all: her cousin's hand in marriage.

One of Vadim's most beautifully realized movies, *Blood and Roses* also demanded some of his most exquisite filming. Georgia's nightmare sequence shot wholly in black and white—and crimson—is spectacular, and Carmilla's "death," impaled on the stake that waits at the end of a dizzying fall, is superbly staged too. But the greatest moment comes with the final few lines—which I will not spoil by repeating here.

THE RAPE OF THE VAMPIRE (*LE VIOL DU VAMPIRE*) (1968)

Sick of movies that make promises that they can't keep? The work of Jean Rollin (1938–2010), described by some as the Russ Meyer of breast-obsessed French fantastical B-movie erotica, will not disappoint in that regard. Two great movies shot at the dawn of his career, the black-and-white *Le Viol du Vampire* (*The Rape of the Vampire*) (1968) and *Le Frisson des Vampires* (*The Shiver of the Vampires*) (1970)—and two more that are at least a lot of fun, *La Vampire Nue* (*The Nude Vampire*) (1970) and *Requiem pour un Vampire* (*Requiem for a Vampire*) (1971)—did much to shock French audiences of the era, paving the way for an enfant-terrible career that may have won few plaudits from serious movie critics but definitely stands high in the world of gratuitous sensationalism. And breasts.

Rape of the Vampire is Rollin's masterpiece, despite being shot on such a minuscule budget that the finished movie was actually two shorts pieced together to make a single feature. The first, which bears the overall title, is the story of four beautiful sisters who live in a remote and crumbling chateau where they are under the control of a ghastly old man who has convinced them that they are vampires. They then overlay this conviction upon their own existing fears and neuroses: one sister was blinded by witch hunters; another was violently raped by the local villagers.

Into this wonderfully atmospheric and deliciously disturbing ménage arrive three Parisian doctors, bent on curing the sisters of what they insist is their imagined vampirism. Rather, the doctors declare, the girls simply fear men.

Their admonishments can only unleash a bloodbath as the old man sets about defending what he sees as his personal playthings. But even he meets his comeuppance in the second of the two films, *Queen of the Vampires*, as the titular monarch arrives to reveal that not only were the sisters' vampiric tendencies utterly bona fide, but one of them was actually preparing a rebellion against the queen's dominion. Cue more gruesome killings, more blood and gore, and naturally, a very unhappy ending.

Critics slammed the movie, and audiences hated it. At a theater in Paris's traditionally open-minded La Pigalle district, enraged moviegoers hurled things at the screen to show their displeasure, and Rollin briefly considered abandoning his movie career there and then. Instead he returned to a similar theme for *La Vampire Nue*.

The action opens with a band of white-coated, red-masked scientists disrobing a maiden to the strains of free-form jazz music, injecting her full of a very nasty-looking cocktail...and then we cut, to find another young lovely being pursued through the suburbs by further masked marauders. Yes, it is all very existential, as you'd expect from French underground cinema of the age, all the more so since so much of the opening action takes place without a word of dialogue.

Eventually, however, we discover that a wealthy industrialist seeking the secrets of immortality has located what he believes to be the answer to his years of research, a mute orphaned vampire whose biochemistry he now intends to pirate. And only the affections of his son, who seems to have fallen in love with the girl, can spoil things.

Nudity, or at least toplessness, is the chosen mode of dress among our industrialist friend's coterie of female employees, and within those confines, *La Vampire Nue* dances merrily along, an unequivocal child of its time that features sufficient clever camera work to justify its avant-garde sensibilities, sufficient soft-core suggestion to confer underground irresponsibility, and just enough suggestion of vampirism—nude vampirism!—to ensure its late-night creature-feature status.

In fact, there are no true vampires in the movie; they were awaiting Rollin's third film, *Le Frisson des Vampires*, a pièce de résistance that tugs upon every vampiric string imaginable. A married couple honeymooning in the company of two sinister servants, former employees of the bride's recently deceased cousins. But they are not deceased. They are vampires....

The fourth and final movie in the series, *Requiem*, is probably the best known of the quartet, in that it swiftly became as infamous overseas as the first in the sequence was at home. A naked whipping scene, shot in the ruined dungeon of a chateau in Crêvecoeur, was one of several that were perforcedly reshot, fully clothed, to get past the objections of foreign censors; a lovemaking sequence, too, was respectfully covered up; and as is so often the case, it was the knowledge of the original scenes, rather than the reality of the reshot ones, that brought *Requiem* a degree of vicarious notoriety around UK and US theaters when it reached those markets. Needless to say, the uncut version is the one to seek out.

(Rollin would return to the vampire theme later in his career, although neither *Les Deux Orphelines Vampires* [1997] nor *La Fiancée de Dracula* [1999] truly compare with the best of his early work.)

LEMORA: A CHILD'S TALE OF THE SUPERNATURAL (1973)

"What are you?" asks the little girl.

"I am whatever you want to be," replies the woman.

We start with a murder, an adulterous couple being mowed down in their bed by the woman's enraged husband. We shift to church, where his daughter Lila Lee (Cheryl Smith) is now a singing angel, entertaining the pious and "washed clean of the evil counsel" of her dead mother and on-the-run father. And we cannot help but wonder, how clean is she really?

A mysterious letter arrives, inviting her to spend time with a woman who claims to know where her father is. Its sender, Lemora (Lesley Gilb), makes no provision for Lila Lee's journey, but she runs away from the church regardless, escaping not only from the strictures of the establishment but from the sexual advances of the minister. There is, however, no escape from licentiousness. She sneaks a ride in a young man's car, only to witness him and his girlfriend making out. She escapes into the city and finds herself dropped into the heart of the red-light district. And when she goes to catch a bus to her final destination, the tiny town of Astaroth, she discovers that the station doesn't sell tickets for that particular ride. You just pay the driver when you board ... with whatever you have that he might want.

Lemora awaits, and in many ways, the unfolding of a plot that is not that easy to discern becomes very secondary to the surrealism of the camera work, all wide-angled lenses and saturated blue tone; to the heightened sexuality that permeates Lemora's domain; to a stylized seductiveness that works as effectively on the viewer as it does on little Lila Lee.

Condemned by the Catholic Legion of Decency on its release, *Lemora* is an ever-gathering miasma of gently unfolding eroticism, softly layered into a universe that seems better adapted to horror. And it plays evenhandedly with both. The rude, empty cell into which she is thrown upon arriving at her destination; the crone who brings Lila Lee her first meal, and sings a ghastly song in a croaking, crackling voice; the gangs of renegade mutants who dwell in the surrounding forests, fighting one another to the death; the mysterious snapping and snarling of the creatures of the night—all stand in vivid contrast to Lila Lee's still-fervent Christian faith, and the mocking laughter that shatters her recitation of the Lord's Prayer is a shock for viewer and victim alike.

And so Lila Lee's discomfort and fear grow exponentially with the hours she is kept locked in her cell with just the crone's occasional visits for company, but when she escapes, it is to discover the truth about Lemora, a black-clad vision of old-world elegance who feeds on the blood of Lila Lee's imprisoned father, and who will now be preparing Lila Lee for her destiny.

Lemora is not classically beautiful, but she is striking: high cheekbones, sunken eyes, pale lips, her hair drawn up tight and her outfit corset-cranked tight. Her home is overrun with playful, cackling children; she serves them blood-red wine. Well, "sort of" wine, Lemora explains. But she dances with Lila Lee, bathes her, laughs with her, and even finds time for a little exposition: how there are two kinds of people in Astaroth, those that are infected by a degenerative disease that ultimately reduces them to a feral, primitive state, and those who are either immune or have been cured.

That is the war that takes place without Lemora's walls—the war, too, that will claim Lila Lee's father's life when he falls prey to the infection. Escaping from Lemora, the girl finds herself on those frontlines, desperately evading the mutant search parties that hunt her with flaming brands and all the tenacity of the peasants who once pursued Frankenstein's monster. When she holes up in a deserted wooden barn, you can almost imagine her meeting a similar fate.

Instead she escapes, to be reunited with Lemora and then with her minister, who has been searching for her too. On this occasion, however, he is gratified to discover that Lila Lee is no longer spurning his advances. She seems willing, even anxious, to kiss him. Which is when we discover that Lemora has given the girl something more than love and affection. And now she must feed.

Lemora: A Child's Tale of the Supernatural is a beautiful movie, haunting and haunted, one of those rare opuses that overcome any physical deficiencies in their creation by force of atmosphere and ambition alone. Lemora herself is as striking a vampire queen as has ever walked among us (as she herself points out as the movie nears its climax), but we are left with the impression that Lila Lee might even eclipse her. Her minister, after all, is only her first victim. The next time we see her, she is back in church, singing like an angel but eyeing the congregation like ... well, like something quite the opposite.

THE HUNGER (1983)

"Would you like some sherry?"

"No, thank you. I really don't like sherry."

"I think you'll like this one."

Even among his most loyal acolytes, few folk would describe David Bowie as one of the twentieth century's most accomplished actors. A genius songwriter and performer he may be, possessed of such powers of conviction that when he first emerged on the major stage in 1972, many people genuinely believed (or wanted to, which amounts to the same thing) that he was a bisexual alien; the creator, too, of a series of personas so immaculate that their very names are as well known as his own: Ziggy Stardust, the Thin White Duke, Aladdin Sane.

On film, however, the mystery and mystique seem to slip away. Playing Thomas Jerome Newton, the man who fell to Earth in Nicolas Roeg's movie of the same name, Bowie is tolerated because he is essentially playing the being we all hoped he really was—a disoriented space alien trying to make sense of this planet. And in *Merry Christmas, Mr. Lawrence*, a sprawling drama set in a World War II Japanese prisoner of war camp, he is believable because his apparent fear and bemusement at the sight of the cameras could easily be translated into the emotions a real-life POW might have felt. Plus, he gets to deliver one of the all-time greatest lines in any modern war movie. "Do you know what I'm thinking?" asks his Japanese interrogator. "No. Do you?" responds Bowie.

Elsewhere, however, Bowie has graced and grafted through more forgettable movies than most people could remember even under torture, but there is one—count them, *one*—in which he not only convinces, he does so without recourse to any gift beyond the one he most infrequently exhibited in his musical career. The ability to actually be himself: a mild-mannered, quietly spoken, reassuringly handsome middle-class Brit.

The Hunger was based on a novel by Texan horror author Whitley Strieber, in which form it comes across as little more than an enjoyable vampiric potboiler. Under the watchful eye of the late director Tony Scott, however, it is transformed into an epic of such sensuality that many reviews condemned it for falling into soft pornographic territory, and doing so with such an absence of apology that you could almost believe not one of them had ever watched or read a single vampire story in the past.

French superstar Catherine Deneuve is Miriam, an ageless vampire beauty whose memories (seen in occasional flashback) date back to the days of ancient Egypt; Bowie plays her lover, John, a three-hundred-year-old Englishman who barely looks one-tenth of his age. Until the awful afternoon when all of those years come piling in at once, transforming him from a sophisticated, urbane hipster who shares his mistress's taste for visiting gothic nightclubs and devouring the losers they take back to their penthouse, into a bitter old bag of resentful sticks who cannot believe he was never warned that this was the fate that awaited him. And then it's up to the attic he goes, to be carefully filed away alongside all of Miriam's other past lovers, while she gets to work seducing her next conquest, a doctor named Sarah (Susan Sarandon). With eternity in which to ponder the fact that everlasting life is not so alluring if you just keep growing older.

Such an absorbing movie, alive with so many visceral highlights. We open with Bauhaus and "Bela Lugosi's Dead," played out with singer Peter Murphy in a cage while the nightclub goes about its business around him. The first kill is delicious, an ankh sliced open to reveal a vicious blade; and later, a louche young lad who thinks he is God's gift to women, bloodily discovering that God is the last person he should be thinking about. Or poor old John, rattling home to the strains of Iggy Pop's "Funtime," and taking his blade to a skater just as Iggy's lyric hits the line about "Dracula and his crew."

Sarandon, as a medical mind studying and attempting to

reverse the effects of aging in apes, plays it magnificently coolly; the moment when she realizes she maybe shouldn't have ignored the old man waiting patiently in her reception area, claiming to have been young that same morning, jolts her so hard that the viewer can almost physically feel it.

Bowie astonishes when, on the point of total physical decay, he snatches at Alice, the teenaged girl who visits Miriam for music lessons, and feasts on her body before casting her corpse aside. And Deneuve, as always, is such a breathtaking presence— innately regal, timelessly beautiful. Her seduction of Sarandon, with a gossamer melody from Léo Delibes's *Lakmé* drifting over the bed, casts an alluring eye back at *Carmilla* but rides, too, a rogue element, medical science wrestling with the truth of vampiric infection.

"There is nothing to be frightened of, so long as you have faith in me."

There are (look away if you haven't seen it yet) a couple of continuity lapses as the movie nears its climax. A suicidal Sarah is not to know that a blade in the neck will not kill her, but Miriam surely does. So why does she carry the woman's blood-soaked body up to the attic to lay with the rest of the nearly departed? And while we do not know what precise mechanism needs to kick in before a vampire will commence the aging process, would a mere fall truly suffice for a twenty-five-hundred-year-old immortal? One to ponder, although thankfully, the mood of *The Hunger* is sufficiently strong that one is carried along by the love, not the logic.

Perhaps the true star of the movie, however, even more than Scott's flawless direction or the career-best performances dealt out by its stars (for Sarandon has never bettered this either), was make-up artist Dick Scott, the man who not only rearranged Bowie's then notoriously less-than-perfect dentition into a smile that any vampire would be pleased to flash, but also worked the cosmetic magic that allowed the star to age three centuries in just a few minutes. Without the makeup ever actually looking like makeup. In a movie genre where pancake flesh, ruby lips, panda-bear mascara, and slicked-back hair are frequently the only talents an aspiring makeup artist needs to have mastered, Smith's epic demolition of the Bowie face and frame was worth every hour the singer must have spent in the makeup chair.

Whitley Strieber, author of the original novel, has since published two sequels pursuing the undead Miriam's adventures. (See appendix B.) Bowie, meanwhile, revisited at least the vampiric subtext of *The Hunger* in the video for his 2013 single "The Stars (Are Out Tonight)."

DRACULA'S WIDOW (1988)

How do you know when you've been bitten by a female vampire?

Well, if it was Dracula's widow who did the deed, she will have left bright red lipstick smeared around the punctures.

Fifteen years after she reigned supreme as the queen of soft-core film, Emmanuelle, Sylvia Kristel reappeared as Vanessa, the nemesis for sundry Hollywood lowlifes, in a movie that looks and feels more like something made for TV in the mid-1970s than conceived on the edge of the final decade of the last century—and is all the more glorious for it. Set in the heart of Hollywood, whose garish neon only adds to the movie's raw retro atmosphere, with the vampiric Vanessa setting up house in an equally antiquated wax house of horrors, *Dracula's Widow* is a startlingly effective piece of work. Super schlocky, but effective.

Especially imaginative is the scene when, having already dispatched a would-be Romeo and an incompetent burglar, Vanessa disturbs the museum's Nicolas Cage–lookalike owner, Raymond, as he watches *Nosferatu* in his bedroom. Movie shadows blend with the widow's own, and though brief, the moment is definitely a great piece of camera work.

Into this bloodbath, meanwhile, there steps the hard-bitten veteran cop whose narration overlays the movie, investigating a growing stream of corpses. "Real hamburger meat," warns his assistant of the sight of the first body; "Get me a picture of him with his face on," is the cop's measured response, although he becomes a little less glib after one of his fellow officers becomes the next victim. Being dragged backward through the station window with claws through the throat is not the most familiar cause of death in a vampire movie, but it definitely does the trick.

A shockingly doddery grandson of the original Van Helsing makes an appearance, enjoying his work even more thoroughly than his ancestor used to. But Vanessa remains the star of the show, imperiously commanding Raymond to do her every bidding, gratuitously carving flesh every time she gets peckish, and inadvertently stumbling upon a nest of murderous Satanists whom she has a high time hacking to very bloody collops.

She also drops the beautiful dame act, and is revealed for no apparent reason as a gruesome hag. Although by this point, nothing is too surprising. Not even Raymond sitting by a pool chowing down on raw fish, while wondering (somewhat naively, at this point) what is happening to him. Not even Van Helsing being turned into a vampire. Or Vanessa turning back from a bat. But sometimes a movie doesn't need to be surprising. It just needs to hold your attention long enough to make you forget how bad some of the special effects are. And *Dracula's Widow* does all of that.

FROM DUSK TILL DAWN (1996)

Encounter a vampire with a name like Santanico Pandemonium, and you probably know things are not going to go your way. But encounter her when you're a pair of psycho killers on the run—having already torched a truck stop, murdered your hostage, and executed a cop—and you probably deserve everything you get.

Escaping Texas after perhaps the ultimate crime spree gone bad, and maintaining the mayhem at a border motel (while playing the horror gore at least partially for laughs), brothers Seth (George Clooney) and Richie (Quentin Tarantino) finally wash up at the Titty Twister, a grubby bar in the deepest wilds of Mexico, neon lit and biker infested, a slice of sleaze supreme.

It also happens to employ the hottest exotic dancer either brother has ever seen (Salma Hayek). Who then transforms into the most terrifying vampire either could imagine, the moment she scents the blood spilled when the brothers get into a bar fight with some local rowdies.

Matters just go downhill from there.

Billed by her employers as "The Mistress of the Macabre, the Epitome of Evil," draped in snakes and dancing through fire, Santanico's onstage demeanor paints her as the ringleader of the vampires. Several other strippers and the house band share her tastes, but Hayek's performance is exquisite (at least before she turns into the half-reptile vampire monster), an epiphany of vampiric fantasies: the seething seducer, the aloof beauty, the ice-cold executioner. This impression is promptly dismissed, of course, by the unrelenting prosthetic ick factor of the fight scene that follows—and the fact that Santanico does not live long enough to make good on her promise to turn Seth into her dog. Who, she says, she will name Spot.

Holed up in a battered bar strewn with body parts, decomposing flesh, and charred goo, half a dozen human survivors (who no longer include Richie, vamped by Santanico before she was dispatched and then staked in turn by his brother) are rapidly chopped down to five … four … three … two … and then the dawn's first rays hit the mirror ball, and the whole place goes up like the Fourth.

A sequel, *From Dusk till Dawn 2: Texas Blood Money*, and a prequel, *The Hangman's Beautiful Daughter*, followed in 1999 and 2000 respectively. Gore hounds will be pleased to learn they maintained the original's bloody body count, if nothing else.

UNDERWORLD (2003)

Until his tragically early death from a congenital heart defect in 1979, Richard Beckinsale was one of Britain's most beloved and effective television comedy stars, a brilliant sidekick to two of the profession's most venerable veterans, Ronnie Barker (the prison-based sitcom *Porridge*) and Leonard Rossiter (*Rising Damp*). Wife Judy Loe, too, was a familiar face on British TV throughout the 1970s and beyond, and while the Beckinsales probably remain small fish in the ocean of acting's great familial dynasties, still the success of their two daughters, Samantha and Kate, would surprise nobody who believes that brilliance can be hereditary.

Kate, born July 26, 1973, was already a slowly rising star when

2001 brought her major roles in the World War II epic *Pearl Harbor* and the comedy *Serendipity*. But it was her appearance in the first installment of the *Underworld* series that confirmed her ascension, as director Len Wiseman stepped behind the barely spoken scenes of every previous vampire and werewolf movie to reveal what those two races do when humans can't see them.

True Blood, of course, tells a somewhat similar story, the two races locked into a centuries-old struggle that merges familial rivalry and clannish ambition with a bloodlust so old that many of the combatants don't even seem to remember why they are at war. They just accept that they are, and so vampire and lycan devote their entire time and energy to seeking new ways of slaughtering one another, while both sides try to perfect the ultimate secret weapon—a purebred cross between the two species.

Beckinsale is Selene, a vampire Death Dealer who, in the first of the movies, becomes involved with Michael Corvin—whom, it rapidly transpires, is that hybrid. Their relationship, and the lengths to which both vampire and lycan hordes will go to end it, forms the heart of the *Underworld* series. The first two movies, *Underworld* and *Underworld: Evolution* appeared in 2003 and 2006 respectively, and together created a fabulous alternate universe, peopled by some of the finest characterizations ever to don either cape or fur. Bill Nighy as the fifteen-hundred-year-old Hungarian warlord Viktor is especially awe inspiring, the actor's natural facial expressions (so effective in the comedy roles for which he is most renowned) becoming an excellent additional weapon in his already impressive arsenal of vampire tics and gymnastics.

Against him, the lycan are led by William Corvinus, the founder of the strain itself and the brother of the vampires' founding father, Marcus. This backstory, which does grow unnecessarily complicated in places (although it's nothing that a good fight scene cannot remedy), informs the third of the *Underworld* movies, the historical prequel, *Underworld: Rise of the Lycans* (2009)—a movie from which Selene is absent, but which nevertheless explains many of the events that dictate all that will befall her in both the first two films and the fourth in the series, 2012's *Underworld: Awakening*.

There is little subtle about the *Underworld* movies. They are, first and foremost, action flicks, with all the kicking, punching, whirling, and whizzing that that genre demands. The traditional traits of both vampires and werewolves are seldom dwelt upon for any length of time, and the sexual tensions that the vamp film now regards as a traditional prerequisite are likewise secondary to the fist fights and gun battles.

But the sets are phenomenal, the mood is pure gothic, and the mythology is at least as believable as any other attempt to explain how and why a fully functioning supernatural community has managed to exist and prosper in the shadows that the human race is too blinkered to explore. And that includes *True Blood*'s intriguing backstory.

Remember, after all, the only proof we have that vampires, werewolves, fairies, and ghosts do *not* exist is that with which we are provided by the same breed of people who once were equally adamant that global warming did not exist. The history of science is actually the history of mankind finally acknowledging (and more importantly, accepting) truths that have been under its nose for centuries beforehand—which in turn demands that any alternate reality that fiction may posit is, in fact, no less likely to be accurate than the accepted sciences that insist they are not.

None of this is intended to portray the events within *Underworld* as anything but a riotous slice of ultraviolent entertainment. But if ever there were a way of lining Selene the vampire up against Buffy the slayer, nobody should be in any doubt as to who would emerge victorious.

Roman Polanski's immortal *The Fearless Vampire Killers* (1967)—truly one of the most uproarious romps in undead movie history. (Author's collection)

11

A-HUNTING WE WILL GO:
OR, A SPLASH OF HOLY WATER...

In October 2004, Sotheby's auction house catalogued, and sold for $26,400, what was described as "a vampire killing kit circa 1900. The walnut box with brass lock and red plush fitted interior contained a wood stake, a double barrel pistol, nine bullets, six bullet cloths, an ivory-mounted wood crucifix, serum and a lidded tin containing powdered flowers of garlic."

Seven years later, a similar kit sold at the same house for an almost equally remarkable $25,000, and visitors to the various Ripley's Believe It or Not "odditoriums" scattered around the world can see up to forty more of these fascinating items on public display.

More lurk on eBay; many more are still being manufactured, or at least fabricated from sundry antique items, today. Vampire killing kits are big business, and have been ever since...

...ever since when? Since Bram Stoker's Van Helsing first went abroad armed with "something like a cricketing bag," filled with the many and varied tools of his trade? Before that, in the wilds of the European East, perhaps; after that, in the golden age of manic merchandising, for certain. According to an investigation in the *Fortean Times* magazine in spring 2012, the earliest printed reference to an actual "real life" vampire killing kit is less than thirty years old, appearing in a *House of Swords and Militaria* mail-order catalog in the mid-1980s.

This is not to say that people were not making, and using, such kits years, decades, or centuries before then. Just that such specialist tools are probably best regarded as the property of specialist workers. People who really do hunt vampires for a living, people who really do need a monogrammed Gladstone bag. People whose name is Van Helsing.

Or Buffy.

Or even the Fellowship of the Sun.

THE GREATEST VAN HELSING OF THEM ALL

Born August 6, 1922, and a star of the English stage long before he made his first inroads into TV and film, English actor Sir Frank Finlay has appeared in so many memorable roles, and absolutely adopted so many fascinating characters, that to pluck his performance in December 1977's BBC adaptation *Count Dracula* from thin air and hold it up as an example of his acting at its best could be seen as mere thematic convenience.

Certainly one could latch onto any of maybe a dozen other Finlay roles and proclaim them his greatest. Iago in Olivier's 1965 *Othello*, Sancho Panza in 1973's *The Adventures of Don Quixote*—Finlay has played roles as far apart as Casanova in the 1971 BBC TV drama of the same name and Hitler in 1973's *The Death of Adolf Hitler*; has journeyed from Marley's ghost in the excellent George C. Scott recounting of *A Christmas Carol* (1984) to the faintly creepy, and certainly overprotective, father in *Bouquet of Barbed Wire* in 1976.

Inspector Lestrade in the Holmes movies *A Study in Terror* and *Murder by Decree*, the immortally titled Witchsmeller Pursuivant in the first season of *Blackadder*, Adrien Brody's father in Polanski's *The Pianist*, and so many, many more—Finlay was knighted for his services to entertainment in 2012. *Dracula*, then, was just one stepping-stone among so many.

Even more damaging to his inclusion here, he did not even appear as a vampire in the BBC production. The role of Dracula fell to Louis Jourdan, with Finlay cast merely as his nemesis, Van Helsing. But with his *Bouquet* costar Susan Penhaligon appearing as Lucy to respark the fabulous chemistry that made the earlier show such a sensation, Finlay was unflinchingly brilliant.

As in the adaptation itself, Finlay's scenes with the count echo the original novel with prepossessing symmetry. Where the actor succeeds beyond any previous portrayal of Van Helsing is in his refusal to acknowledge any of the clichés that generally cling to the old man. Finlay's character is fanatical in his devotion to his calling, but he is not so driven that he overlooks, or at least glosses over, the human toll.

Even Peter Cushing, traditionally regarded as the archetypal Van Helsing, pales alongside Finlay's performance, and for the first time, we see Dracula and Van Helsing as two sides of the same coin, a yin-yang conundrum in which one needs the other almost as validation of his own existence. Only Sherlock Holmes and Moriarty (and possibly Doctor Who and the Master) could claim to have painted a similar relationship so vibrantly, and it seems incredible that *Dracula* should have waited until its eightieth anniversary before openly revealing that side of the story.

But of course, it was always there if you searched.

It is only in recent years that either literature or cinema has made a hero of the vampire hunter. Prior to that, the role was almost exclusively the preserve of a near-fanatical zealot who saw evil and blood thirst in everyone he met, and was capable of the most appalling feats of ineptitude in his quest to rid the world of the evil taint.

True, some remarkable actors have played the role: John Gottowt in Murnau's *Nosferatu*, Edward Van Sloan in Universal's *Dracula* and *Dracula's Daughter*, Peter Cushing throughout the Hammer sequence, Herbert Lom in 1969's *Count Dracula*, Laurence Olivier in 1979's *Dracula*, Anthony Hopkins in *Bram Stoker's Dracula*.

But until Finlay came along, our sympathy was never with Van Helsing, or whatever nom de guerre his archetype appears under, and that might be why nobody ever really bothered with dedicating a movie to *his* adventures. Well, *almost* nobody.

THE FEARLESS VAMPIRE KILLERS, OR PARDON ME, BUT YOUR TEETH ARE IN MY NECK (1967)

Coming off the success of *Repulsion*, truly one of the most terrifying horror movies ever made, and sandwiched between *Cul-de-Sac* and *Rosemary's Baby* in Roman Polanski's filmography, *The Fearless Vampire Killers* (a.k.a. *Dance of the Vampires*) is often regarded as the idiot bastard son of the director's golden years.

It is a comedy, shot at a time when few people expected such a beast from Polanski. And it is so heavily in thrall to the Universal pics of thirty years before that even the crew engaged for the production apparently regarded it as "old-fashioned nonsense" (or so cinematographer Douglas Slocombe told Ivan Butler, author of *The Cinema of Roman Polanski*). But watch with an unjaundiced eye and it is an unforgettable romp, beautifully shot and costumed, and directed with no less passion than Polanski expended on his better-regarded movies.

Every cliché in the vampire book is employed, knowingly and delicately. Polanski explains in his *Roman by Polanski* autobiography, "Our basic aim was to parody the genre in every way possible while making a picture that would, at the same time, be witty, elegant, and visually pleasing."

Alfie Bass's Jewish vampire's disdain for crucifixes has already been remarked upon here, but similar jewels litter the landscape. Even the naming of the primary vampire, Count Von Krolock (Ferdy Mayne), is a playful tribute to Max Schreck's character in *Nosferatu*, while the dance sequence (!) at the movie's conclusion was not only borrowed from Hammer, it was devised by Norwegian choreographer Tutte Lemkow, the "fiddler on the roof" in the movie of the same name.

Polanski, playing Alfred, the younger of the movie's eponymous heroes, possesses an onscreen earnestness that delights in every scene he appears in, while Sharon Tate (destined to become Polanski's wife and so horribly murdered by the Manson gang in 1969) imbibes the role of the innkeeper's daughter with a sexuality that is positively tangible. Again, her reputation as one of the rising stars of late-1960s Hollywood is largely predicated upon her roles in more "serious" movies (a very brief but, if you spot her, memorable cameo in her husband's *Rosemary's Baby* and an utterly vivacious starring role in *Valley of the Dolls* among them). But *The*

Fearless Vampire Killers had no time for reputation, and emerged all the more powerful because of it.

The sets are spectacular. Filming took place high in the Dolomite mountains of Italy, on a snowy plateau called Valgardena near the ski resort of Ortisei. A castle was built there, just one element in an extravagant layout that really does look and feel authentic. Plus, it was the height of winter, and nature obliged with lashings of snow—not for nothing had Polanski engaged Roy Stevens as his assistant director. A few years earlier, Stevens worked on the similarly winter-bound *Doctor Zhivago*.

Yet the precious jewel we see on DVD today is not that which was originally released in the US. Polanski describes any number of niggling problems with the studio as *The Fearless Vampire Killers* came together, ranging from the censorial objection to the phrase "I'll stick it somewhere up you" to one exec's insistence that Sharon Tate apparently had the ghost of a mustache in her naked bathtub scene. Polanski promptly wrote back, "You will be even more alarmed to know that she is also growing a pair of balls."

But worse was to come, as the movie's US distributors slashed twenty minutes from its running time and then redubbed the remainder with American voice actors. Outraged, Polanski tried first to have his name removed from the credits, only to discover that his contract forbade it. So he took to the media to complain about the treatment, and when MGM warned him to stop or risk "never working in this town again," he took that threat to the media too.

The Fearless Vampire Killers was lost on release; it "sank without trace," as Polanski put it. "It was only years later, as my version was released around the world, that it became successful as something of a cult film."

BUFFY THE VAMPIRE SLAYER (1992)

Destined to spin off one of the most successful supernaturally themed shows in television broadcast history—and therefore, the granddaddy of the next two-decades-plus worth of vampire entertainment—*Buffy the Vampire Slayer* started life as a not-especially-applauded teen movie starring Kristy Swanson as the eponymous Buffy; Donald Sutherland as Merrick, the watcher charged with recruiting her to her stake-hauling destiny; and Rutger Hauer as Lothos, the local king of the vampires.

It's tremendous fun in a brainless kind of way, a wild ride through a series of scares, thrills, and comic interludes that establishes all the ground rules for the eventual television phenomenon—primarily that Buffy is the Slayer, ordained by fate to continue the age-old battle against the scourge of vampirism. Disturbing dreams dating back as far as she can remember are the evidence of that; now the dreams are reality, and Buffy takes to her new role with bloodthirsty alacrity.

This is not to say that creator Joss Whedon was necessarily happy with Hollywood's treatment of his Valley-girl cheerleading heroine, nor that he would not make several substantial revisions to the movie's backstory once *Buffy the Vampire Slayer* moved into televisual production.

The phenomenon that is Buffy (and, of course, the spin-off *Angel*) would not look back. The basic premise, however, remained unchanged. Her name is Buffy and she slays vampires.

VAN HELSING (2004)

The critics hated it; audiences adored it. And historians positively swoon over it. *Van Helsing* was so deeply indebted to the Universal movies of the 1930s that the opening sequence even looks like one.

Both the Wolfman and Frankenstein's monster lumber in alongside Drac in a movie that doesn't *quite* hit all the right buttons (the business about Van Helsing being the Archangel Gabriel is especially dumb, and Richard Roxburgh plays an especially hammy count). But it does rattle along at a remarkable pace, all the more if you watch it in two separate sittings, rather than try and sit through the full two hours at once. And while we might ask what could there possibly be left to say about the most famous vampire hunter of them all that had not already been said by over a century's worth of past writings, movies, and reimaginings, *Van Helsing* doesn't even try to answer the question. Why should it?

Van Helsing is very much a return to vampire (and other) hunting as it ought to be done, with an action-man hero (Hugh Jackman) who is part Indiana Jones, part Rambo, part James Bond (complete with his own Vatican-approved Q), and only marginally related to the often error-prone gent who had born the name Van Helsing in the past.

Certainly it opens dramatically, with the moments leading up to the presumed death of the Frankenstein monster in the pyre of a blazing windmill, while Dracula and his brides look on in something resembling dismay. And all lavishly shot in a black-and-white hue that instantly transports the viewer back to the original movies.

Then cut to Paris, where we are introduced to Van Helsing, striving to fulfill the demands of the Vatican's Knights of the Holy Order by capturing Doctor Jekyll and Mr. Hyde. It's a dramatic (and gag-strewn) sequence that acquaints us with the hero's resourcefulness just in time for him to be charged with his next quest: to destroy Dracula, and at the same time redeem the soul of the last living member of the Valerious family, Anna, whose family had undertaken a similar holy pledge nine hundred years earlier and was now doomed to purgatory until the task was completed.

And cue one of those delightful moments when Hollywood reminds us just how schizophrenic this acting game can be. Anna Valerious, sworn foe of the vampires, looks, sounds, and moves identically to Selene, *Underworld*'s queenly vampire Death Dealer.

But not to worry: Kate Beckinsale, for it is she, is as believable as a vampire hunter as she was on the other side of the battlefield, and so *Van Helsing* rocks and rolls along so good-naturedly excitingly that you want to snap the pencil of all of the critics who advised you against going to see the movie. And then stab them through the heart with the stump.

DEMONS (2009)

British television's answer to Buffy from the people who brought you *Hex* (see chapter 5), *Demons* follows the adventures of Luke Rutherford, a guileless teen who suddenly discovers that he is the last of the legendary Van Helsing family line, tasked by destiny to rid the world of not only vampires but any demon that should assault the planet. It's a mantle that Buffy had long since made her own, of course, and *Hex*'s Ella Dee (the irresistible Laura Pyper) had raised to even greater heights with her battle against the nephilim. And doubtless that familiarity worked against Luke in terms of captivating a TV audience. So did the absurdly unrealistic American accent adopted by actor Philip Glenister in the role of Luke's godfather, mentor, and hoary old demon-smiter in his own right.

But let us not cast stones at all that was … not *wrong*, but not quite right either … about the show. *Demons* rocks like a mutha, from its hypercatchy theme (the Starlight Mints' "Eyes of the Night") onward. And if Luke's quest to rid the planet—or at least his corner of London—of demons seems a little overwhelming for a teenaged boy and a hard-drinking pseudo-Texan, help is at hand. Please welcome Ruby, Luke's not-so-easily-frightened girlfriend; and one other supernatural agent, a blind vampiric concert pianist who turns out to be *Dracula*'s Mina Harker. Whose son, Quincy, is the target of the team's most bloody encounter with another vampire.

Other foes include a cannibalistic harpy; a half-man, half-rat genius; and an ancient demon who survives by devouring the life force of passing children. Ingenious enemies, indeed, and ones that conspired to raise *Demons* a lot higher up the must-see TV totem than its meager one-season/six-episode lifespan might normally suggest.

A detective and her vampire sidekick—oh, and her partner, the patsy. *Blood Ties* (2007–2008) was one of twenty-first-century television's greatest vamp love affairs … so far. (Author's collection)

12

THEY'RE CREEPY AND THEY'RE KOOKY: A BRIEF HISTORY OF TELEVAMPIRE VISION

THE ADDAMS FAMILY (1964–1966)

It's hard to believe, given how many vampires have made their homes on the TV schedules of the twenty-first century, that such things were actually a rarity throughout most of the twentieth. Hard to believe, too, that those that did happen along tended to blaze but fast and glorious before being condemned to the cancellation bin.

We look back at the superlative success of *True Blood*, and its popularity now feels preordained. But if you had told a TV executive of ten, twenty years ago that a vamp-based series could survive five seasons, with more still to come, he'd have looked at you as though you were Renfield. And then staked you out in the sunshine for a while.

The Addams Family is the archetypal American family unit. Mom and dad, two kids and a pet, the grandparents always on hand for emergencies, and of course, the slightly weird uncle who keeps getting into scrapes. It's a formula that has dominated sitcoms since the dawn of the genre. With one exception. This time, they're all dead.

No, that's wrong. Some of them *may* be dead. Uncle Fester, for example. The one who looks like a well-fed zombie, with sunken eyes and a fiendish grin. Pugsley, the son, is alive right now, but only because his sister Wednesday hasn't yet perfected the ideal means of dispatching him. Lurch, the butler, was undoubtedly constructed from the cast-off body parts of who-knows-how-many corpses? And, of course, there's Morticia. Lean, saturnine, strikingly beautiful, devastatingly elegant, and prone to speaking in French, the language of lovers, whenever English feels too coarse to convey her true intentions. Oh, and she's a vampire.

The Addams Family was created, as its name suggests, by cartoonist Charles Addams, originally as a cartoon series drawn for *The New Yorker* between 1938 and his death fifty years later, but exploding into multimedia prominence courtesy of television, cinema, video games, and even a musical.

Which is how the vampire made its television debut—by not being especially vampiric whatsoever. Not in *The Addams Family*, which hit the screens in 1964; nor in *The Munsters*, which adopted much the same premise that very same year, and bedazzled every viewer with a lifelong running joke lifted directly out of *I Am Legend*. In a household filled with horror movie staples, the normal human (the vampiric Lily's niece Marilyn) is the freak.

I have noted elsewhere in this book that, throughout much of the middle of the twentieth century, the classic creatures of cinematic horror had been reduced to little more than a tired joke. Alongside *Dark Shadows*, the gothic soap that made a superstar of Barnabas Collins, *The Addams Family* and *The Munsters* must shoulder some of the blame for that weariness.

Although that doesn't change the fact that all three were brilliant, and all three have been made into enjoyable recent feature films too.

THE NIGHT STALKER (1971)

Notwithstanding the television adaptation of Stephen King's *'Salem's Lot* and the inevitable late-night reruns for sundry classic movies, "serious" vampires would very much lurk below television's radar throughout much of the medium's first fifty years. There would occasionally be a bad vamp protagonist turning up in the midst of another show's story line, and the peculiar aspect of that fact is, they tended to be cop and/or detective dramas. Two fields that, the occasional Holmesian red herring aside (and Tod Browning's *London After Midnight*, a 1927 epic in which a detective *disguises* himself as a vampire) had rarely coincided in the past.

It was a 1971 TV movie, *The Night Stalker*, that set up the scenario that has, as we shall soon see, become the undead's most potent role on the small screen. Investigating a series of grisly serial killers around the Las Vegas Strip, newspaper reporter Carl Kolchak (Darren McGavin) comes to the conclusion that the murderer is either a vampire or believes himself to be one. Of course it is not a story that will fly past his hard-bitten editor, Anthony Vincenzo, and so Kolchak is left to his own devices, at least until he can persuade the police that they are battling with the supernatural.

With a teleplay by *I Am Legend* author Richard Matheson, and destined to land the highest-viewing figures yet earned by a television movie, *The Night Stalker* spawned both a sequel and a terrific TV series, as well as finally winning publication for the novel that inspired it—Jeff Rice's *The Kolchak Papers* had languished unwanted by every publisher in the land until the author's agent decided to pitch it instead to television. The novel, retitled for the movie, appeared in 1974, the year after the second movie, *The Night Strangler*, paired Kolchak with a less-than-vampiric but nonetheless bloodthirsty killer in the darkness of Seattle's underground city.

The TV series, meanwhile, survived just twenty of the intended twenty-six episodes, as low ratings and even lower critical opinions sent it limping to an early grave. Its impact, however, would not be as minimal. Not only has *The Night Stalker* been cited among the formative influences on *The X-Files*, it also forged a whole new genre for both television and species: the vampire detective.

FOREVER KNIGHT (1992)

Nicholas Knight (Geraint Wyn Davies) is an eight-hundred-year-old vampire, a former French knight who tires of the centuries of murder and mayhem he has hitherto enjoyed and decides to utilize his talents for good. He joins the Toronto police department and lands a job as detective on the night shift. A rare skin condition is his excuse for never being seen in the office by daylight, and his vow to never again feed on humans is maintained by a diet of bottled animal blood—which, we soon discover from the response of other vamps in the city, is a fairly disgusting habit.

Running for three seasons, 1992 to '96, *Forever Knight* was a reasonable romp, albeit one that often allowed the police work to take precedence over its supernatural elements. Nevertheless, it was sufficiently well received that Canadian television would step back into the same waters a little over a decade later with the debut of *Blood Ties*, a similarly themed series based upon author Tanya Huff's Blood Books series of novels.

KINDRED: THE EMBRACED (1996)

Fans of *Kindred* insist that eight episodes are by no means enough time for a show to truly arrive at its full potential. Critics argue that if you can't figure out your story line in two months, you probably never will. Either way, *Kindred: The Embraced* is one of the great nearly-was adventures of 1990s TV, the story of a San Francisco cop, Frank Kohanek (C. Thomas Howell), who suddenly discovers that the city is teeming with vampires.

The Kindred, as they call themselves, are bound beneath the rule of a prince, Julian Luna (Mark Frankel), who just happens to be the mob boss whom Kohanek is investigating. This sets up a dilemma that very few cops can have ever faced before. Kohanek can continue with his duty and bust the mob boss, in which case the various factions within the Kindred will shatter and unleash a horde of hungry vampires upon the innocent city. Or he can ally himself with the bad guy, and join him in policing both human and vampire criminality.

Among the handful of reviews that did not damn *Kindred: The Embraced* to an early grave were several that compared it, in terms of plotting at least, to *The Godfather.* Which isn't that bad a recommendation. Sadly, however, we will never discover just how the whole mess was ever to be resolved. Or whose bed the horse's head would wind up in.

ULTRAVIOLET (1998)

A six-part British TV series, *Ultraviolet* starts out as yet another law enforcement drama, as Detective Sergeant Michael Colefield (Jack Davenport) goes in search of his partner, Jack (Stephen Moyer), who mysteriously vanished on the night before his wedding. The mystery takes a violent turn, however, when Colefield uncovers a top-secret government department dedicated to hunting vampires—whom most rational people naturally believed were a thing of fiction alone. Even more shocking is the discovery that Jack has himself been transformed into a vamp, but retains just enough of his old humanity and sense of duty to have joined the hunters.

With a mere six episodes in which to tell the story, *Ultraviolet* is fast paced enough to be almost dizzying, beautifully filmed and very well acted, and certainly overflowing with shocks. Just don't, *please* don't, confuse it with the movie of the same name.

BLOOD TIES (2007)

Tanya Huff's novels established the premise of the show. A 470-year-old vampire named Henry Fitzroy is known to the world as the author of a series of successful historical romances (and, less famously, is a hitherto unknown son of King Henry VIII of England). Vicki Nelson, meanwhile, is an Ontario cop forced into retirement by her worsening eyesight. Now she works as a private detective, and six novels published throughout the 1990s (*Blood Price*, *Blood Trail*, *Blood Lines*, *Blood Pact*, *Blood Debt*, and the short-story collection *Blood Bank*) follow the adventures that the pair share through the city's hitherto unsuspected occult underground.

Two television series, amounting to twenty-two episodes total, were produced throughout 2007–2008, with Kyle Schmid's performance as Fitzroy powerful enough to land him high on sundry "sexiest vampire" style polls. In terms of storytelling, too, *Blood Ties* is distinguished by a genuinely gritty feel and a delightfully tight tension between its main characters. Fitzroy and Nelson's undeniable mutual attraction is complicated by the attentions of her former lover and partner Mike Celluci—an arch cynic who is more concerned that Vicki is losing her marbles, imagining all this occult nonsense, than he is by the possibility that the city is under siege from an army of werewolves, demons, zombies, and more.

Maybe he should have asked for a transfer to Bon Temps. Or to Los Angeles, where even as *Blood Ties* was seducing viewers north of the border, *Moonlight* was allowing an American vampire to join the crime-fighting carousel.

MOONLIGHT (2007–2008)

Not to be confused with *Moonlighting*, which was the story of two all-too-human private detectives; or *Blood Ties*, which married a private detective to a vampire; or even *The Dresden Files*, in which a professional wizard finds himself serving as an unofficial assistant to a certain kind of police investigation; US television's *Moonlight* was the story of a vampire private detective, Mick St. John (Alex O'Loughlin), who falls in love with newspaper reporter Beth (Sophia Myles) while on the trail of one particular case.

Naturally there are complications, not least of all in the form of his ex-wife and maker, Coraline (Shannyn Sossamon), who has apparently returned from destruction in the hope of picking up where she and St. John left off.

In terms of vampirism, St. John is still a rookie. He was turned a mere half century ago, although his circle of acquaintances does include the four-hundred-year-old Josef, a successful businessman; and Logan Griffen, a vampire computer hacker. St. John's work as a private eye also engages him with a succession of other night stalkers, most of whom have nefarious ends that only he, with his understanding of their habits and motives, can crack.

Sadly, the 2007–2008 Writers Guild of America strike planted a stake firmly through St. John, figuratively if not literally (stakes are surprisingly nonlethal to *Moonlight*'s vampires; fire and silver are their only true foes), and after much humming and hawing and mixed signals from the publicity department, *Moonlight* was canned with just sixteen episodes made.

British actress Myles returned to the UK following *Moonlight*'s cancellation, where her future roles intriguingly included another character named Beth in the ninth season of the BBC's acclaimed spy drama *Spooks*—in which America's favorite British vampire date was supplanted, for season 10, by the woman destined to become Sookie Stackhouse's favorite British fairy godmother, the superlative Lara Pulver.

DARK SHADOWS (2012)

On television, the saga of *Dark Shadows* captivated generations for five years (1966–1971), four of which were dominated by the vampire Barnabas Collins (Jonathan Frid). Broadcast every weekday for a total 1,225 episodes, *Dark Shadows* spun off two movies during 1970–1971 (*House of Dark Shadows* and *Night of Dark Shadows*), a short-lived 1991 TV remake, an even shorter-lived (pilot episode only) 2004 revisitation, and a 2006 audio drama series.

Most recently, however, there is the 2012 Tim Burton blockbuster that casts Johnny Depp as Barnabas Collins, transformed into a vampire by the witch Angelique and then imprisoned for the next two hundred years. He is finally freed in 1972 and returns home to discover his descendants are somewhat less deserving of a proud family name than he would have preferred.

Once one of America's most powerful and wealthy families, the Collinses now merely rattle around the decaying gothic remains of a splendid family seat: "The place was designed for a staff of a hundred," the disenchanted footman tells the newly arrived nanny (Bella Heathcote). "Now it has a staff of me." Two hundred rooms are largely closed off ("to save on heating," explains the family matriarch Elizabeth Collins Stoddard— Michelle Pfeiffer), meals are eaten in confrontational near-silence, and the kids are revolting.

Into this dysfunctional drama Barnabas is reborn, fresh from draining the construction crew who inadvertently freed him, and naturally ripe for a few moments of bemusement as he walks through the modern-day town and gazes uncomprehendingly at motor cars, pizza joints, and record stores. Family introductions follow, but so does an even less welcome one—to the equally well-preserved Angelique, and the reopening of the warring that caused so much pain and suffering in the past.

In terms of characterization and special effects, *Dark Shadows* the movie is a welcome successor to the TV of fond memory. One just wishes that a better story line had been arrived at. The internecine conflict between a couple of rival seafood canning companies in New England would scarcely sustain a business seminar, let alone the rebirth of one of America's most beloved bloodsuckers.

Oh well, maybe there'll be a sequel.

Nosferatu ahoy! And people wonder why sailors are so superstitious!
(Author's collection)

Epilogue

Two thousand years of legend, two thousand years of horror, two thousand years of romance. Vampires are not only one of humanity's longest-surviving night terrors, they are also one of the best documented. And whether you believe in their existence or not, the fact that you have reached the end of this book, and probably been diverted by at least a handful of movies, comics, songs, and novels, suggests that you would *like* to believe.

And so you should. The world would be very boring indeed if we only believed in the things that we have incontrovertible proof of, and dismissed as phantasms all that lies beyond. Why shouldn't a secret community of vampires, werewolves, and faeries and fiends exist in the shadows beyond the corners of our eyes? That is, after all, what *secret* means, and the fact that no one has conclusively stumbled upon its existence just proves that *some* species are better at keeping their mouths shut than *others*.

That was the world before *True Blood* came along; that *is* the world as it unfolds in *Underworld*, and that is the story of *Ночной дозор* (*Nochnoy Dozor*), or *Night Watch* (2004), a spellbinding Russian production that begins where the universe normally ends, with the final battle between good and evil. Only in this instance, the battle took place in the distant past, with a frightful conflict to which, both sets of combatants realized, there could be no victor. So they called a truce, policed by officials from both sides of the divide, invisible to man, unknown to his institutions. The good hunt down the evildoers, the evil neutralize the do-gooders.

Until...

These guardians are everywhere, and they could be anyone. The butcher at the market, the garbagemen cleaning streets, the guy riding the subway beside you. Which is reassuring until you realize this means the transgressors they seek could be anyplace too. That kid on the sidewalk, the cop on the beat, the girl in the centerfold.

It's a complex movie, or at least fast moving enough that if you don't pay attention you will miss something that might prove integral later. We learn the characters' qualities as the movie progresses, and the nature of the war as well. We meet vampires that can be seen only by flashlight, and that explode into porcelain when reflected light strikes them.

But there are things even worse than vampires lurking in modern Moscow: the fulfillment of an age-old prophecy, and the search for the one thing that can prevent it from coming to pass. That is the true story of *Night Watch*, and it is one that will engross you for sure. Because regardless of whether or not vampires and everything else exist; regardless of whether or not myth and legend are simply the ghosts of a memory that civilization and science have spent centuries quashing; regardless, even, of just how far we are willing to suspend our belief; one fact remains.

If there were no such things as vampires and werewolves, changelings and fairies, ghosties and ghoulies and long-legged beasties and things that go bump in the night...

...someone would have invented them.

ACKNOWLEDGMENTS

Thanks go out to everybody who lent a hand with this book, from Amy Hanson on the home front, who nobly endured a three-month festival of Hammer horror films, to everyone at Hal Leonard, including copyeditor Joanna Dalin and editor Jessica Burr, who brought the beast to life.

To Linda and Larry, Karen and Todd, Jo-Ann Greene, Dave and Sue, Gaye and Tim, Princess Jen, Bateerz and family, Oliver and Toby and Trevor, Barb East, Geoff Monmouth, and everyone else who threw a suggestion into the pot; to Mick Farren, Rozz Williams, Dave Vanian, Peter Murphy, Daniel Ash, Steve Severin, Nico and Siouxsie, and everyone else whose voice is heard in this book; and to Him and/or Her Out of Thingy, cast members in so many of the movies and TV shows that were viewed with a view toward recalling why I love them.

THE TOP TEN

1. *Nosferatu* (1922)
Director: F. W. Murnau
Stars: Max Schreck, Greta Schröder, Ruth Landshoff, Gustav von Wangenheim

2. *Black Sunday* (1960)
Director: Mario Bava
Stars: Barbara Steele, John Richardson, Andrea Checchi, Ivo Garrani

3. *Blood and Roses* (1960)
Director: Roger Vadim
Stars: Mel Ferrer, Elsa Martinelli, Annette Vadim, Alberto Bonucci

4. *The Fearless Vampire Killers* (1967)
Director: Roman Polanski
Stars: Jack MacGowran, Roman Polanski, Alfie Bass, Jessie Robins

5. *Lemora: A Child's Tale of the Supernatural* (1973)
Director: Richard Blackburn
Stars: Cheryl Smith, Leslie Gilb, Maxine Ballantyne, William Whitton

6. *Martin* (1976)
Director: George A. Romero
Stars: John Amplas, Lincoln Maazel, Christine Forrest, Elyane Nadeau

7. *The Hunger* (1983)
Director: Tony Scott
Stars: Catherine Deneuve, David Bowie, Susan Sarandon, Cliff De Young

8. *Shadow of the Vampire* (2000)
Director: E. Elias Merhige
Stars: John Malkovich, Willem Dafoe, Udo Kier, Cary Elwes

9. *Underworld* (2003)
Director: Len Wiseman
Stars: Kate Beckinsale, Scott Speedman, Shane Brolly, Michael Sheen

10. *Let the Right One In* (2008)
Director: Tomas Alfredson
Stars: Kåre Hedebrant, Lina Leandersson, Per Ragnar, Henrik Dahl

THE GOLDEN OLDIES

11. *Dracula* (1931)
Director: Tod Browning
Stars: Bela Lugosi, Helen Chandler, David Manners, Dwight Frye

12. *Vampyr* (1932)
Director: Carl Theodor Dreyer
Stars: Julian West, Maurice Schutz, Rena Mandel, Sybille Schmitz

13. *Mark of the Vampire* (1935)
Director: Tod Browning
Stars: Bela Lugosi, Lionel Barrymore, Elizabeth Allen, Carole Borland

14. *Dracula's Daughter* (1936)
Director: Lambert Hillyer
Stars: Otto Kruger, Gloria Holden, Edward Van Sloan

15. *Son of Dracula* (1943)
Director: Robert Siodmak
Stars: Lon Chaney Jr., Evelyn Ankers, George Irving, Louise Allbritton

16. *House of Dracula* (1945)
Director: Erie C. Kenton
Stars: Lon Chaney Jr., John Carradine, Martha O'Driscoll, Lionel Atwill

17. *Isle of the Dead* (1945)
Director: Mark Robson
Stars: Boris Karloff, Ellen Drew, Marc Cramer, Katherine Emery

18. *The Vampire's Ghost* (1945)
Director: Lesley Selander
Stars: John Abbott, Charles Gordon, Peggy Stewart, Grant Withers

19. *El Vampiro* (1957)
Director: Fernando Mendez
Stars: Abel Salazar, Ariadne Robies, Carmen Montejo, German Robles

20. *The Return of Dracula* (1958)
Director: Paul Landres
Stars: Francis Lederer, Norma Eberhardt, Ray Stricklyn, Jimmie Baird

THE HAMMER YEARS

21. *Dracula* (US title *Horror of Dracula*) (1958)
Director: Terence Fisher
Stars: Peter Cushing, Christopher Lee, Michael Gough, Melissa Stribling

22. *The Brides of Dracula* (1960)
Director: Terence Fisher
Stars: Peter Cushing, David Peel, Martita Hunt, Yvonne Monlaur

23. *The Kiss of the Vampire* (1963)
Director: Don Sharp
Stars: Noel Willman, Edward de Souza, Clifford Evans, Jennifer Daniel

24. *Dracula: Prince of Darkness* (1966)
Director: Terence Fisher
Stars: Christopher Lee, Francis Matthews, Barbara Shelley, Philip Latham

25. *Dracula Has Risen from the Grave* (1968)
Director: Freddie Francis
Stars: Christopher Lee, Rupert Davies, Barbara Ewing, Veronica Carlson

26. *Taste the Blood of Dracula* (1970)
Director: Peter Sasdy
Stars: Christopher Lee, Geoffrey Keen, Gwen Watford, Madeleine Smith

27. *Scars of Dracula* (1970)
Director: Roy Ward Baker
Stars: Christopher Lee, Dennis Waterman, Jenny Hanley, Christopher Matthews

28. *The Vampire Lovers* (1970)
Director: Roy Ward Baker
Stars: Ingrid Pitt, George Cole, Kate O'Mara, Peter Cushing

29. *Lust for a Vampire* (1971)
Director: Jimmy Sangster
Stars: Ralph Bates, Michael Johnson, Barbara Jefford, Yutte Stensgaard

30. *Countess Dracula* (1971)
Director: Peter Sasdy
Stars: Ingrid Pitt, Lesley-Anne Down, Nigel Green, Sandor Eles

31. *Twins of Evil* (1971)
Director: John Hough
Stars: Inigo Jackson, Judy Matheson, Peter Cushing, Harvey Hall

32. *Daughters of Darkness* (1971)
Director: Harry Kümel
Stars: Delphine Seyrig, John Karlen, Danielle Ouimet, Andrea Rau

33. *Dracula A.D. 1972* (1972)
Director: Alan Gibson
Stars: Christopher Lee, Peter Cushing, Christopher Neame, Stephanie Beacham

34. *Vampire Circus* (1972)
Director: Robert William Young
Stars: Adrienne Corri, Thorley Walters, Anthony Higgins, John Moulder-Brown

35. *The Satanic Rites of Dracula* (1973)
Director: Alan Gibson
Stars: Christopher Lee, Peter Cushing, Joanna Lumley, Michael Coles

36. *Captain Kronos: Vampire Hunter* (1974)
Director: Brian Clemens
Stars: Horst Janson, John Cater, Caroline Munro, Ian Hendry

THE '70S

37. *The Body Beneath* (1970)
Director: Andy Milligan
Stars: Gavin Reed, Jackie Skarvellis, Berwick Kaler, Susan Heard

38. *The Night Stalker* (1971)
Director: John Llewellyn Moxey
Stars: Darren McGavin, Simon Oakland, Carol Lynley

39. *Blacula* (1972)
Director: William Crain
Stars: William Marshall, Vonetta McGee, Denise Nicholas, Gordon Pinsent

40. *Scream Blacula Scream* (1973)
Director: Bob Kelljan
Stars: William Marshall, Pam Grier, Don Mitchell, Michael Conrad

41. *Vampira* (1974)
Director: Clive Donner
Stars: David Niven, Teresa Graves, Nicky Henson, Jennie Linden

42. *Blood for Dracula* (a.k.a. *Andy Warhol's Dracula*) (1974)
Director: Paul Morrissey
Stars: Joe Dallesandro, Udo Kier, Vittorio De Sica, Maxime McKendry

43. *Mrs. Amworth* (1975)
Director: Alvin Rakiff
Stars: Glynis Johns, Roger Davidson, Derek Francis, Rex Holdsworth

44. *Zoltan: Hound of Dracula* (1978)
Director: Albert Band
Stars: Michael Pataki, Jose Ferrer, Jan Shutan, Libbie Chase

45. *Nosferatu the Vampyre* (1979)
Director: Werner Herzog
Stars: Klaus Kinski, Isabelle Adjani, Bruno Ganz, Roland Topor

46. *Love at First Bite* (1979)
Director: Stan Dragoti
Stars: George Hamilton, Susan Saint James, Richard Benjamin, Arte Johnson

47. *Thirst* (1979)
Director: Rod Hardy
Stars: Chantal Contouri, Shirley Cameron, Max Phipps, Henry Silva

THE FILMS OF THE BOOKS

48. *The Last Man on Earth* (1964)
Director: Ubaldo B. Ragona
Stars: Vincent Price, Franca Bettoia, Emma Danieli, Giacomo Rossi-Stuart

49. *Dracula* (1979)
Director: John Badham
Stars: Frank Langella, Laurence Olivier, Donald Pleasence, Kate Nelligan

50. *'Salem's Lot* (1979)
Director: Tobe Hooper
Stars: David Soul, James Mason, Lance Kerwin, Bonnie Bedelia

51. *Bram Stoker's Dracula* (1992)
Director: Francis Ford Coppola
Stars: Gary Oldman, Winona Ryder, Anthony Hopkins, Keanu Reeves

52. *Interview with the Vampire: The Vampire Chronicles* **(1994)**
Director: Neil Jordan
Stars: Brad Pitt, Tom Cruise, Antonio Banderas, Kirsten Dunst

53. *I Am Legend* (2007)
Director: Francis Lawrence
Stars: Will Smith, Alice Braga, Charlie Tahan, Salli Richardson-Whitfield

THE '80S

54. *Fright Night* **(1985)**
Director: Tom Holland
Stars: Chris Sarandon, William Ragsdale, Amanda Bearse,
Roddy McDowall

55. *Near Dark* **(1987)**
Director: Kathryn Bigelow
Stars: Adrian Pasdar, Jenny Wright, Lance Henriksen, Bill Paxton

56. *The Lost Boys* **(1987)**
Director: Joel Schumacher
Stars: Jason Patric, Corey Haim, Dianne Wiest, Barnard Hughes

57. *Nosferatu a Venezia* **(a.k.a.** *Vampire of Venice*) **(1988)**
Director: Augusto Caminito
Stars: Klaus Kinski, Donald Pleasence, Christopher Plummer, Barbara De
Rossi

58. *Dracula's Widow* **(1988)**
Director: Christopher Coppola
Stars: Sylvia Kristel, Josef Sommer, Lenny von Dohlen, Marc Coppola

59. *Sundown: The Vampire in Retreat* **(1989)**
Director: Anthony Hickox
Stars: David Carradine, Morgan Brittany, Bruce Campbell, Jim Metzler

THE '90S

60. *Tale of a Vampire* (1992)
Director: Shimako Sato
Stars: Julian Sands, Suzanna Hamilton, Kenneth Cranham, Marian Diamond

61. *Innocent Blood* (1992)
Director: John Landis
Stars: Anne Parillaud, Anthony LaPaglia, Robert Loggia, David Proval

62. *Cronos* (1993)
Director: Guillermo del Toro
Stars: Federico Luppi, Ron Perlman, Claudio Brook, Margarita Isabel

63. *Blood and Donuts* (1995)
Director: Holly Dale
Stars: Gordon Currie, Louis Ferreira, Helene Clarkson, Fiona Reid

64. *The Addiction* (1995)
Director: Abel Ferrara
Stars: Lili Taylor, Christopher Walken, Annabella Sciorra, Edie Falco

65. *From Dusk till Dawn* (1996)
Director: Robert Rodriguez
Stars: Harvey Keitel, George Clooney, Juliette Lewis, Quentin Tarantino

66. *Blade* (1998)
Director: Stephen Norrington
Stars: Wesley Snipes, Stephen Dorff, Kris Kristofferson, N'Bushe Wright

67. *John Carpenter's Vampires* (1998)
Director: John Carpenter
Stars: James Woods, Daniel Baldwin, Sheryl Lee, Maximilian Schell

THE MODERN VAMPIRE

68. *Trouble Every Day* (2001)
Director: Claire Denis
Stars: Vincent Gallo, Tricia Vessey, Béatrice Dalle, Alex Descas

69. *Dracula: Pages from a Virgin's Diary* (2002)
Director: Guy Maddin
Stars: Wei-Qiang Zhang, Tara Birtwhistle, David Moroni, Cindy Marie Small

70. *Blade II* (2002)
Director: Guillermo del Toro
Stars: Wesley Snipes, Kris Kristofferson, Ron Perlman, Leonor Varela

71. *Vampires: Los Muertos* (2002)
Director: Tommy Lee Wallace
Stars: Jon Bon Jovi, Natasha Gregson, Arly Jover, Diego Luna

72. *Night Watch* (2004)
Director: Timur Bekmambetov
Stars: Konstantin Khabenskiy, Vladimir Menshov, Mariya Poroshina, Valeriy Zolotukhin

73. *Vampires: The Turning* (2005)
Director: Marty Weiss
Stars: Colin Egglesfield, Stephanie Chao, Roger Yuan, Patrick Bauchau

74. *Frostbitten* (2006)
Director: Anders Banke
Stars: Petra Nielsen, Grete Havnesköld, Carl-Åke Eriksson, Emma Åberg

75. *Day Watch* (2006)
Director: Timur Bekmambetov
Stars: Konstantin Khabenskiy, Mariya Poroshina, Vladimir Menshov, Galina Tyunina

76. *Perfect Creature* (2006)
Director: Glenn Standring
Stars: Dougray Scott, Saffron Burrows, Leo Gregory, Scott Wills

77. *Underworld: Evolution* (2006)
Director: Len Wiseman
Stars: Kate Beckinsale, Scott Speedman, Derek Jacobi, Bill Nighy

78. *30 Days of Night* (2007)
Director: David Slade
Stars: Josh Hartnett, Melissa George, Danny Huston, Ben Foster

79. *Thirst* (2009)
Director: Chan-wook Park
Stars: Kang-ho Song, Ok-bin Kim, Hae-suk Kim, Ha-kyun Shin

80. *Strigoi* (2009)
Director: Faye Jackson
Stars: Catalin Paraschiv, Rudy Rosenfeld, Constantin Barbulescu, Roxana Guttman

81. *Underworld: Rise of the Lycans* (2009)
Director: Patrick Tatopoulos
Stars: Bill Nighy, Michael Sheen, Rhona Mitra, Kevin Grevioux

82. *The Countess* (2009)
Director: Julie Delpy
Stars: Julie Delpy, Daniel Brühl, William Hurt, Anamaria Marinca

83. *We Are the Night* (2010)
Director: Dennis Gansel
Stars: Karoline Herfurth, Nina Hoss, Jennifer Ulrich, Anna Fischer

84. *Stake Land* (2010)
Director: Jim Mickle
Stars: Connor Paolo, Nick Damici, Kelly McGillis, Gregory Jones

85. *Let Me In* (2010)
Director: Matt Reeves
Stars: Kodi Smit-McPhee, Chloë Grace Moretz, Richard Jenkins, Cara Buono

86. *Fright Night* (2011)
Director: Craig Gillespie
Stars: Anton Yelchin, Colin Farrell, David Tennant, Toni Collette

87. *Midnight Son* (2011)
Director: Scott Leberecht
Stars: Shawn-Caulin Young, Tracey Walter, Arlen Escarpeta, Larry Cedar

88. *Dark Shadows* (2012)
Director: Tim Burton
Stars: Johnny Depp, Michelle Pfeiffer, Helena Bonham Carter

89. *Abraham Lincoln: Vampire Hunter* (2012)
Director: Timur Bekmambetov
Stars: Benjamin Walker, Rufus Sewell, Dominic Cooper, Anthony Mackie

90. *Underworld: Awakening* (2012)
Directors: Måns Mårlind and Björn Stein
Stars: Kate Beckinsale, Sandrine Holt, Theo James, Michael Ealy

EROTICA AND XXX

91. *The Rape of the Vampire* (1968)
Director: Jean Rollin
Stars: Solange Pradle, Bernard Letrou, Catherine Deville, Ursule Pauly

92. *The Nude Vampire* (1970)
Director: Jean Rollin
Stars: Christine François, Olivier Rollin, Maurice Lemaître, Ursule Pauly

93. *The Shiver of the Vampires* (1970)
Director: Jean Rollin
Stars: Sandra Julien, Jean-Marie Durand, Jacques Robiolles, Michel Delahaye

94. *Requiem for a Vampire* (1971)
Director: Jean Rollin
Stars: Marie-Pierre Castel, Mireille Dargent, Philippe Gaste, Louise Dhour

95. *Vampyres* (1974)
Director: José Ramón Larraz
Stars: Anulka (Playboy's Miss May 1973), Marianne Morris, Murray Brown, Brian Deacon

96. *Gan Shi Yan Tan* (*Ghoul Sex Squad*—a.k.a. *Kung Fu Vampire Killers*) (1991)
Director: Mah Wu Tu
Stars: Chiao-Niang Chin, Nioa-Wang Lan, Mei-Chiao Lin, Lo-Pa

97. *Ritual* (2008)
Director: Marc Dorcel
Stars: Claudia Rossi, Jennifer Love, Jennifer Lowe, Gina

98. *Lesbian Vampire Killers* (2009)
Director: Phil Claydon
Stars: Paul McGann, James Corden, MyAnnas Buring
Note: Don't be put off by either the title or the categorization. This movie is funny!

99. *Tru: A XXX Parody* (2010)
Director: Lee Roy Myers
Stars: James Deen, Misty Stone, Ashlynn Brooke, Evan Stone

100. *Buffy the Vampire Slayer XXX: A Porn Parody* (2012)
Director: Lee Roy Myers
Stars: Jessie Andrews, Tom Byron, Rocco Reed, Lexi Belle

APPENDIX B:
100 GREATEST VAMPIRE NOVELS AND SERIES

INDIVIDUAL NOVELS

1. *Absence of Faith: A Vampire's Lesson in Betrayal*—E. Carter Jones (iUniverse, 2000)
2. *Afterage*—Yvonne Navarro (Overlook Connection Press, 1993)
3. *Ancestral Hungers*—Scott Baker (Tor Books, 1995)
4. *Bad Blood*—Pat Whitaker (Trafford Publishing, 2007)
5. *The Bat*—Mary Roberts Rinehart (Dell Books, 1954)
6. *Bent Steeple*—G. Wells Taylor (self published, 2009)
7. *Bitter Things*—Andrew Valentine (National Writers Press, 2009)
8. *Blood Born*—Linda Howard and Linda Jones (Ballantine Books, 2010)
9. *Blood Groove*—Alex Bledsoe (Night Shade, 2006)
10. *Blood Is Thicker Than Water*—Wynette A. Hoffman (Alien Perspective Paperback, 2002)
11. *The Blood of Kings*—John Michael Curlovich (Alyson Books, 2005)
12. *The Blood of the Covenant*—Brent Monahan (St. Martin's Paperbacks, 1995)
13. *The Blood of the Goddess*—William Schindler (Xlibris Corp., 2001)
14. *Blood of the Templar*—D. H. Nations (Double Dragon Publishing, 2009)
15. *Bloodshift*—Garfield Reeves-Stevens (Popular Library, 1990)

16. *Bloodsucking Fiends: A Love Story*—Christopher Moore (Simon & Schuster, 1995)

17. *Blood to Blood: The Dracula Story Continues*—Elaine Bergstrom (Ace, 2000)

18. *Blue Dawn Over Gettysburg: A Supernatural Tale of Union Victory*—Joe DeSantis (Trafford Publishing, 2008)

19. *The Book of Common Dread*—Brent Monahan (St. Martin Press, 1994)

20. *Bound in Blood: The Erotic Journey of a Vampire*—David Thomas Lord (Kensington Books, 2001)

21. *Bring On the Night*—Don and Jay Davis (Tor Books, 1993)

22. *Carmilla: A Vampyre Tale*—J. Sheridan Le Fanu (1872)

23. *Code Blood*—Kurt Kamm (MCM Publishing, 2011)

24. *Curse of the Vampire*—David A. Wilson (PublishAmerica, 2003)

25. *Daughter of Darkness*—Steven Spruill (St. Martin's Press, 1999)

26. *Daughters of the Moon*—Joseph Curtin (Pinnacle, 2000)

27. *Dawn of the Vampire*—William Hill (Pinnacle, 2001)

28. *Daylight*—Elizabeth Knox (Harper Perennial, 2003)

29. *Death by the Drop*—Timothy Massie (BookSurge Publishing, 2008)

30. *The Delicate Dependency: A Novel of the Vampire Life*—Michael Talbot (Avon Books, 1982)

31. *Descendant: Chronicles of the Ipswich Witch*—Miranda Bachman (CreateSpace, 2011)

32. *A Discovery of Witches*—Deborah E. Harkness (Penguin Books, 2011)

33. *Dracula*—Bram Stoker (Archibald Constable and Company, 1897)

34. *Dracula: A Symphony in Moonlight and Nightmares*—Jon J. Muth (NBM Publishing Co., 1993)

35. *Dracula the Un-Dead: The Sequel to the Original Classic*—Dacre Stoker and Ian Holt (Dutton/Penguin, 2009)

36. *Enter, Night*—Michael Rowe (ChiZine Publications, 2011)

37. *Facade of Shadows*—Rick Chiantaretto (American Book Publishing, 2006)

38. *Fevre Dream*—George R. R. Martin (Poseidon Press, 1982)

39. *Good Lady Ducayne*—Mary Elizabeth Braddon (1896)
40. *H.M.S. Vanguard: A Tale of Horror*—John Conrad (Xlibris Corp., 2003)
41. *The Hunger*—Whitley Strieber (William Morrow, 1981)
42. *I Am Legend*—Richard Matheson (Fawcett Publications, 1954)
43. *The Journal of Edwin Underhill*—Peter Tonkin (Hodder & Stoughton, 1981)
44. *Kindred: The Embraced*—John Gideon (Jove, 1996)
45. *The Last Vampire*—Whitley Strieber (Pocket Books, 2001)
46. *The Letters of Mina Harker*—Dodie Bellamy (University of Wisconsin Press, 2004)
47. *Let the Right One In: A Novel*—John Ajvide Lindqvist (St. Martin Griffin, 2004)
48. *Lilith's Dream: A Tale of the Vampire Life*—Whitley Strieber (Pocket Books, 2002)
49. *Live Girls*—Ray Garton (Pocket Books, 1996)
50. *Lost Souls*—Poppy Z. Brite (Abyss Books, 1992)
51. *Miss America*—Chrissie Bentley (CreateSpace, 2012)
52. *Monastery*—Patrick Whalen (Pocket Books, 1988)
53. *Mozart's Blood*—Louise Marley (Kensington, 2010)
54. *Night Players*—P. D. Cacek (Design Image Group Inc., 2001)
55. *Nocturnas*—Shawn Ryan (Pocket Books, 1995)
56. *Nosferatu: A Novel*—Jim Shepard (Bison Books, 2005)
57. *The Old Power Returns*—Morven Westfield (Harvest Shadows Publications, 2007)
58. *Past Sins*—Don Ecker (Dark Realm Press, 2004)
59. *Reflections of a Vampire*—Damion Kirk (Rahu Books, 2002)
60. *Rulers of Darkness*—Steven Spruill (St. Martin's Press, 1998)
61. *'Salem's Lot*—Stephen King (Signet Books, 1975)
62. *Secret History of Elizabeth Tudor, Vampire Slayer*—Lucy Weston (Gallery, 2010)
63. *Some of Your Blood*—Theodore Sturgeon (Carroll & Graf, 1961)
64. *The Summoning*—Bentley Little (Pinnacle, 1993)
65. *The Sun Will Find You*—Chris Muffoletto (Virtual Publications, 2001)

66. *Tepes*—Johann Wolfe Heisey (PublishAmerica, 2006)
67. *Thirst*—Pyotyr Kurtinski (Leisure Books, 1995)
68. *Vamped: A Novel*—David Sosnowski (Downtown Press, 2004)
69. *VampireS*—John Steakley (Pocket Books, 1990)
70. *Vampire's Waltz*—Thomas Staab (Crazy Wolf Publishing, 2000)
71. *The Vampyre*—John Polidori (1819)
72. *Varney the Vampire, or The Feast of Blood*—variously attributed to either James Malcolm Rymer or Thomas Preskett Prest (1847)

SERIES

73. Almost Human series—Melanie Nowak (2008–date)
74. American Vampire series—Scott Snyder and Rafael Albuquerque (2010–date)
75. Anno Dracula series—Kim Newman (1992–date)
76. Black Dagger Brotherhood—J. R. Ward (2005–date)
77. Blood Books series—Tanya Huff (1991–1997)
78. Buffy the Vampire Slayer novels—various authors (1998–date)
79. Casa Dracula series—Marta Acosta (2006–2010)
80. Chicagoland Vampires—Chloe Neill (2009–date)
81. Dark Ink Chronicles—Elle Jasper (2010–date)
82. Darkwing Chronicles—Savannah Russe (2005–2008)
83. Diaries of the Family Dracul Trilogy—Jeanne Kalogridis (1994–1996)
84. Erotic Vampire series—edited by Cecilia Tan (1994–date)
85. Immortality Bites series—Michelle Rowen (2012–date)
86. Knights of the Darkness Chronicles—D. N. Simmons (2004–2010)
87. Last Vampire/The Thirst series—Christopher Pike (1994–date)
88. Marquis de Sade vampire series—Mary Ann Mitchell (1999–2005)
89. Morganville Vampires series—Rachel Caine (2006–date)
90. Necroscope Saga—Brian Lumley (1986–1991)

91. New Tales of the Vampires—Anne Rice (1998–1999)
92. Renquist Quartet—Mick Farren (1996–2002)
93. Saint-Germain Chronicles—Chelsea Quinn Yarbro (1979–2009)
94. Southern Vampire (Sookie Stackhouse) series—Charlaine Harris (2001–2013)
95. Stone Masters Vampire series—V. M. K. Fewings (2007–date)
96. Texas Vampire series—Diane Whiteside (2006–2008)
97. Vampire Chronicles—Anne Rice (1976–2003)
98. Vampire Plagues series—Sebastian Rooke (2005–2006)
99. Vampires of New England series—Inanna Arthen (2007–date)
100. WVMP Radio series—Jeri Smith-Ready (2008–date)

APPENDIX C:
A NIGHT AT FANGTASIA: 150 MORE SONGS
FROM THE *TRUE BLOOD* SOUNDTRACK

1. "A Drink with Hank"—Sean Patrick McGraw
2. "Ain't Life Hell"—Hank Cochran and Willie Nelson
3. "Ain't No Invisible Man"—Jakob Dylan
4. "All Night Through"—The Shaker Sisters
5. "Always a Friend"—Alejandro Escovedo feat. Bruce Springsteen
6. "And the World Laughs with You"—Flying Lotus feat. Thom Yorke
7. "And When I Die"—The Heavy
8. "Anyone but You"—Sean Patrick McGraw
9. "Back to the Crossroads"—Todd Snider
10. "Bad Blood"—Beck
11. "Beautifully Broken"—Gov't Mule
12. "Before the Night Is Over"—Jerry Lee Lewis feat. B. B. King
13. "Beneath Contempt"—Flesh Field
14. "Between You and I"—Stoll Vaughn
15. "Blame It on the Fact That I'm a Man"—The Mears Brothers
16. "Bleeding Love"—Leona Lewis
17. "Blessa"—Toro Y Moi
18. "Blood"—The Band of Skulls
19. "Blood Like Lemonade"—Morcheeba
20. "Brand New Cadillac"—Wayne Hancock
21. "Broken Bodies"—Acumen

22. "Burning Down the House"—The Used
23. "Bye Bye Little Angel"—Elton Anderson
24. "Child's Play"—Dave Pezzner
25. "Cold, Grey Light of Dawn"—Nick Lowe
26. "Coming for You"—Grant Langston
27. "Crazed Country Rebel"—Hank Williams III
28. "Crazy Like Me"—Camp Burnette
29. "Damned if I Do"—Jace Everett
30. "Dead and Gone"—Los Infernos
31. "Deadcat Rumble"—Zombie Ghost Train
32. "Deeper into You"—Johnny Hazzard
33. "Destiny Complete"—The Angel and Mystic
34. "Devastation Road"—eBlues Highway
35. "Devil in Me"—Ken Will Morton and the Wholly Ghosts
36. "Devil Woman"—Marty Robbins
37. "Die Slow"—Health
38. "Dixie Rocks"—Derrick Procell
39. "Dogs of Hell"—Jason Novak
40. "Do You Remember"—La Luna
41. "Drivin' Nails in My Coffin"—Those Darlins
42. "Dyin' Ain't the End of the World"—The Shake
43. "Dynamite and Whiskey"—Fred Eaglesmith
44. "Escape from Dragon House"—Dengue Fever
45. "Feel Alright"—Steve Earle
46. "Evil Is Going On"—Jace Everett and C. C. Adcock
47. "Evil Ways"—The Hampton (Rock) Quartet
48. "Faith"—Alejandro Escovedo
49. "Family Man"—Craig Campbell
50. "Frenzy"—Screamin' Jay Hawkins
51. "Fresh Blood"—The Eels
52. "Gasoline and Matches"—Buddy and Julie Miller
53. "Gator Blues"—Willie Arons and Joey Peters
54. "Gaz Hilarant"—Brian Jonestown Massacre
55. "Good Behaviour"—Powersolo
56. "Hang It Up"—The Ting Tings
57. "Hard Hearted Hannah"—Dolly Kay

58. "Heebie Jeebies"—The Boswell Sisters
59. "Hell's Bells"—Cary Ann Hearst
60. "Here in This Nowhere Town"—Agona Hardison
61. "Hitting the Ground"—Gordon Gano feat. P. J. Harvey and Frank Ferrer
62. "Hopeless"—Percy Mayfield
63. "Howlin' for My Baby"—M. Ward
64. "How to Become Clairvoyant"—Robbie Robertson
65. "I Gotta Right to Sing the Blues"—Billie Holliday
66. "I Will Rise Up"—Lyle Lovett
67. "I Wish I Was the Moon"—Neko Case
68. "I'm Alive and On Fire"—Danko Jones
69. "Keep This Party Going"—The B-52s
70. "Lawd Have Mercy"—El Camino
71. "Lay Back Down"—Eric Lindell
72. "Let's Boot and Rally"—Iggy Pop and Bethany Cosentino
73. "Lines on the Road"—Kristin Diable
74. "Louisiana Hot Sauce"—Sammy Kershaw
75. "Make Some Noise"—John Etkin-Bell and Mike Farmer
76. "Meet Me in the Alleyway"—Steve Earle
77. "Mexico"—The Spares
78. "Monster Mash"—Boris Pickett and the Crypt-Kickers
79. "Moonlight Remembers"—APM
80. "Necroplasm Fix"—Horrorfall
81. "Never Let Me Go"—Katie Webster
82. "New World in My View"—Sister Gertrude Morgan and King Britt
83. "Night on the Sun"—Iron Horse
84. "Nobody Nowhere"—The Jezabels
85. "No Place to Hide"—Betty Everett
86. "Nothing but the Blood"—Randy Travis
87. "Nowhere"—G. DaPonte
88. "Nowhere to Go"—uncredited
89. "Oh My My"—Michael Mazochi
90. "On a Fast Moving Train"—The Great Crusades
91. "On the Horizon"—John Lincoln Wright

92. "One Monkey Don't Stop the Show"—Sonny Terry
93. "One of Them Days"—Jesse Dayton
94. "Over the Moon"—Jonny Savarino
95. "Pistol Whip Me Back into Your Arms"—Acumen Nation
96. "Play with Fire"—Cobra Verde
97. "Pocket Change"—Alabama Shakes
98. "Power" (Voodoo Version)—King Britt Presents Sister Gertrude Morgan
99. "Reflections"—Joel Evans and Friends
100. "Rescue"—Echo and the Bunnymen
101. "Restraining Order Blues"—Michelle Malone
102. "Rhythm Bound"—Steve Byers
103. "Ride My Train"—Jonathan Clark
104. "Rockin' Bones"—Ronnie Dawson
105. "Rodeo Queen"—Gayle Lynn
106. "Run Like Hell"—Cydney Robinson
107. "Sadie Don't Throw Me Over"—James Combs
108. "Save Yourself"—Stabbing Westward
109. "Scratches"—Debbie Davis
110. "Sex and Candy"—Marcy Playground
111. "Shake and Fingerpop"—Junior Walker and the All Stars
112. "Sleep Isabella"—Abney Park
113. "Sleep Walk"—Henri René
114. "Slither Thing"—Collide
115. "Slow Movin' Man"—The Chillun
116. "Smalltown Banjo Breakdown"—Thomas Richard Smith Sr.
117. "Smokestack Lighting"—Howlin' Wolf
118. "So Far, So Good"—Jim Bianco
119. "Soul of Fire"—Witch
120. "Spell of Wheels"—Peter Case
121. "Spoonful"—Howlin' Wolf
122. "Straight into a Storm"—Deer Tick
123. "Stray Dog"—Kevin Welch
124. "Sunset"—Stevie Wonder
125. "Supreme Illusion" (Nickodemus Remix)—Thievery Corporation

126. "Swampblood"—The Legendary Shack Shakers
127. "Tears Will Be the Chaser for Your Wine"—Wanda Jackson
128. "There Ought to Be a Moonlight Savings Time"—Guy Lombardo
129. "Till You Lay Down Your Heavy Load"—Eilen Jewell
130. "Town Called Heartbreak"—Patti Scialfa
131. "Trains Gonna Roll"—Bastard Sons of Johnny Cash
132. "Train Wreck"—Deanna Johnston
133. "Trash the Place"—See Spot Kill
134. "Trouble"—Jackie DeShannon
135. "Twisting Wind"—Helen Henderson
136. "Vamp Vamp"—James Combs
137. "Waiting 'Round to Die"—Townes Van Zandt and Calvin Russell
138. "Waitin' on the Sky"—Steve Earle
139. "Walkin' in the Shadow of the Blues"—Little Charlie and the Nightcats
140. "Whatever I Am, You Made Me"—Koko Taylor
141. "When the Fire Starts to Burn"—uncredited
142. "Where Did You Sleep Last Night"—Jim Oblon
143. "Whiskey's Gone"—The Zac Brown Band
144. "Who Needs Forever" (Thievery Corporation Remix) —Astrud Gilberto
145. "Wolf Blood Honey"—The Upside Down
146. "You Need Love"—Muddy Waters
147. "You're Gonna Miss Me"—13th Floor Elevators
148. "You're So Mean"—Biff Scarborough
149. "You Smell Like Dinner"—Jinx Titanic and Super 8 C*m Shot
150. "Zombie for Your Love"—Kim Jenz and the Jaguars

BIBLIOGRAPHY

Ashley, Leonard R. N. *The Complete Book of Vampires.* Barricade
  Books, 1998.

Barber, Paul. *Vampires, Burial, and Death: Folklore and Reality*, reprint
  ed. Yale University Press, 1990.

Bartlett, Wayne and Flavia Idriceanu. *Legends of Blood: The Vampire
  in History and Myth.* Praeger, 2006.

Belford, Barbara. *Bram Stoker: A Biography of the Author of Dracula.*
  Knopf, 1996.

Bhalla, Alok. *Politics of Atrocity and Lust: The Vampire Tale as a
  Nightmare History of England in the Nineteenth Century.* Stoius Inc.,
  1990.

Boot, Andy. *Fragments of Fear: An Illustrated History of British Horror
  Films.* Creation Books, 1996.

Bunson, Matthew. *The Vampire Encyclopedia.* Gramercy, 2000.

Carter, Margaret L. *Shadow of a Shade: A Survey of Vampirism in
  Literature.* Gordon Press, 1975.

Codrescu, Andrei. *The Blood Countess: A Novel.* Simon & Schuster,
  1995.

Davison, Carol Margaret. *Bram Stoker's Dracula: Sucking Through the
  Century, 1897–1997.* Dundurn Press, 1997.

Dreyer, Carl Theodor and Christen Jul. *Writing Vampyr.* The
  Criterion Collection, 2008.

Dundes, Alan. *The Vampire: A Casebook.* University of Wisconsin
  Press, 1998.

Dunn-Mascetti, Manuela. *Vampire: The Complete Guide to the World of
  the Undead*, reprint ed. Penguin Studio, 1994.

Edwards, Larry. *Bela Lugosi: Master of the Macabre.* Mcguinn & Mcguire, 1997.

Eisner, Lotte H. *The Haunted Screen.* University of California Press, 1969.

Feeney, F. X. and Paul Duncan, eds. *Roman Polanski.* Taschen, 2006.

Florescu, Radu and Raymond T. McNally. *Dracula, Prince of Many Faces: His Life and His Times.* Little Brown & Co., 1990.

Florescu, Radu and Raymond T. McNally. *In Search of Dracula: The History of Dracula and Vampires,* rev. ed. Mariner Books, 1994.

The Fortean Times, various issues. Dennis Publishing, 1973–2013.

Gibson, Matthew. *Dracula and the Eastern Question: British and French Vampire Narratives of the Nineteenth-Century Near East.* Palgrave MacMillan, 2006.

Gordon, Mel. *The Seven Addictions and Five Professions of Anita Berber, Weimar Berlin's High Priestess of Depravity.* Feral House, 2006.

Guiley, Rosemary Ellen and J. B. MacAbre. *The Complete Vampire Companion.* Hungry Minds, Inc., 1994.

Haining, Peter. *A Dictionary of Vampires.* Robert Hale Ltd., 2001.

Hearn, Marcus. *The Hammer Vault: Treasures from the Archives of Hammer Films.* Titan Books, 2011.

Heldreth, Leonard G. and Mary Pharr. *The Blood Is the Life: Vampires in Literature.* Popular Press, 1999.

Hillen, John Sean. *Digging for Dracula.* Dracula Transylvanian Club Ireland, Ltd., 1997.

Horton, George. *Home of Nymphs and Vampires: The Isles of Greece.* Kessinger Publishing, 2003.

Hull, David Stewart. *Film in the Third Reich: A Study of the German Cinema 1933–1945.* University of California Press, 1969.

Ludlam, Harry. *A Biography of Dracula: The Life Story of Bram Stoker.* W. Foulsham, 1962.

Masters, Anthony. *The Natural History of the Vampire.* A Berkley Book, 1972.

McNally, Raymond T. *Dracula Was a Woman: In Search of the Blood Countess of Transylvania.,* rev. ed. McGraw-Hill, 1987.

Martinez, Gerald, Diana Martinez, and Andres Chavez. *What It Is...What It Was! The Black Film Explosion of the '70s in Words and Pictures.* Hyperion Books, 1998.

Maxford, Howard. *Hammer, House of Horror: Behind the Screams.* Overlook Press, 1996.

Melton, J. Gordon. *Vampire Book: The Encyclopedia of the Undead,* 2nd ed. Visible Ink Press, 1998.

The Monster Times, various issues. The Monster Times Publishing Company, 1972–1975.

Nuzum, Eric. *The Dead Travel Fast: Stalking Vampires from Nosferatu to Count Chocula.* Thomas Dunne, 2007.

Pitt, Ingrid. *The Ingrid Pitt Bedside Companion for Vampire Lovers.* B. T. Batsford Ltd., 1998.

Prawler, S. S. *Caligari's Children: The Film as Tale of Terror.* Da Capo Press, 1980.

Rickels, Laurence A. *The Vampire Lectures.* University of Minnesota Press, 1999.

Rigby, Jonathan. *English Gothic: A Century of Horror Cinema.* Reynolds & Hearn Ltd., 2000.

Silver, Alain and James Ursini. *The Vampire Film: From Nosferatu to True Blood,* 4th ed. Limelight Editions, 2011.

Skal, David J. *Vampires: Encounters with the Undead.* Black Dog & Leventhal Pub., 2001.

Summers, Montague. *The Vampire in Lore and Legend.* Dover Publications, 2001.

Thompson, Dave. *Bayou Underground: Tracing the Mythical Roots of American Popular Music.* ECW Press, 2010.

Thompson, Dave. *The Dark Reign of Gothic Rock: In the Reptile House with the Sisters of Mercy, Bauhaus and the Cure.* Helter Skelter Publishing, 2002.

Thorne, Tony. *Countess Dracula: The Life and Times of Elisabeth Báthory, the Blood Countess.* Bloomsbury, 1997.

Treptow, Kurt W. *Vlad III Dracula: The Life and Times of the Historical Dracula.* Center for Romanian Studies, 2000.

Twitchell, James B. *The Living Dead: A Study of the Vampire in Romantic Literature.* Duke University Press Books, 1981.

Williamson, Milly. *The Lure of the Vampire: Gender, Fiction and Fandom from Bram Stoker to Buffy the Vampire Slayer*. Wallflower Press, 2005.

Wright, Dudley. *Vampires and Vampirism: Legends from Around the World (Classics of Preternatural History)*, reissue ed. Lethe Press, 2001.

INDEX